HD
58.6
.S74
1989

Steele, Paul, 1947-

It's a deal.

$17.95

DATE			

It's a Deal
A practical negotiation handbook

Paul Steele, BA, F. Inst. P.S.
John Murphy, BA, MA, MCIM, M. Inst. P. S., MBIM
Richard Russill, BSc, PhD, M. Inst. P. S.

McGRAW-HILL BOOK COMPANY

London · New York · St Louis · San Francisco · Auckland · Bogotá
Guatemala · Hamburg · Lisbon · Madrid · Mexico · Montreal · New
Delhi · Panama · Paris · San Juan · São Paulo · Singapore · Sydney
Tokyo · Toronto

Published by
McGRAW-HILL Book Company (UK) Limited
Shoppenhangers Road, Maidenhead, Berkshire, SL6 2QL, England
Telephone 0628 23432
Fax 0628 35895

British Library Cataloguing in Publication Data
Steele, Paul T.
It's a Deal
1. Business negotiation
I. Title   II. Murphy, John   III. Russill, Richard
658.4"5
ISBN 0-07-707161-1

Library of Congress Cataloging-in-Publication Data
Steele, P. T. (Paul T.), 1947–
  It's a deal: a practical negotiation handbook / P. T. Steele,
J. H. Murphy, R. C. Russill.
    p.   cm.
  ISBN 0-07-707161-1
  1. Negotiation in business.   I. Murphy, J. H. (John H.), 1934– .
II. Russill, R. C. (Richard C.), 1943– .   III. Title.
HD58.6.S74   1989
658.4—dc20   89–13497

1234 B & S 8909

Typeset by Eta Services (Typesetters) Ltd, Beccles, Suffolk
and printed and bound in Great Britain by Billing & Sons Limited, Worcester

Contents

Preface

The business climate will become progressively more volatile as we move through the 1990s, and it is already becoming obvious that those who survive and prosper will be those who know how to negotiate with confidence.

The climate is already hotting up. The consequences of mistakes made during dealing and negotiating are now devastating. Equally, the rewards for success can be enormous. As competition further squeezes profit margins, the difference between good and bad deals becomes more slender. The negotiator of the 1990s will be walking an economic tightrope. Market conditions are changing so quickly that there is seldom time for a second chance, for a second bite at a mishandled negotiation. A fumbled opening gambit, for instance, can easily wreck a deal. It's a pressure-cooker job which demands highly specialized skills.

We, the authors of this book, are specialist negotiators with many years' experience of leading negotiating teams around the world, of trouble-shooting client companies and governments out of crises. Between us we have run more than 1000 seminars on negotiation.

We have frequently witnessed golden business opportunities squandered as unskilled negotiators have taken the wrong approach, failed to capitalize on another party's error, even just spoken at the wrong moment. Researchers will find few source references in this work: our material is largely original, based on our personal experiences gained at conference tables around the world.

Our aim has been to write a working handbook for busy negotiators, concentrating on how you can improve your performance and improve the deals you make. Checklists have been included, and question-and-answer sections have been used to help you to check on your progress.

Finally, we should like to thank Linzi Henry, Simply Fun, Sheffield for the cartoons, and Allan Lee, Newcastle for assistance with drafts.

Paul Steele
John Murphy
Richard Russill

1

Introducing the process of negotiation

1.1 Who are the negotiators?

While few of us would see ourselves as 'professional' negotiators, the reality is that we all negotiate, and we do it far more than we think. At home, at work, in our social lives, we have to reach agreements with others. Through negotiation we satisfy our personal and our business goals and we settle our differences.

At times, negotiation can be a tricky or delicate process, for reaching agreement usually means that at least one party will have to shift from its original position.

Some people believe that good negotiators are born and not made. It's not true. Good negotiation demands putting effectively into practice a range of skills and a series of different approaches. Acquiring these skills and approaches is not easy. But those who do will reap considerable rewards by winning a better deal in all aspects of life.

Negotiation is not new. We've been using it for thousands of years as a non-violent and socially acceptable way of reaching agreement, of settling our differences.

The American author Herb Cohen told us: 'Your real world is a giant negotiating table, and like it or not, you're a participant.'

There is a remarkable amount of confusion about what negotiation is. So before exploring the methods, techniques and ploys involved, and deciding where they should be used, it's necessary to agree a definition.

1.2 What is negotiation?

A look first of all at some of the more popular definitions of negotiation will illustrate some of the confusion surrounding the process.

"THE NEGOTIATION PROCESS IS A LONG ESTABLISHED MEANS TO REACH AGREEMENT"

- A give-and-take trading process by which the conditions of a transaction are agreed and acted upon.
- Negotiation involves an attempt by two or more parties to complete a transaction through the use of bargaining.
- To negotiate is to confer with another party or parties for the purpose of coming to an agreement.

Other commonly used phrases in connection with negotiation suggest that people meet in order to:

- confer and exchange views;
- come to compromise agreement;
- bargain or trade with each other through give and take.

Newspaper headlines regularly confuse the meaning of negotiation. They mix up 'discussions' with 'negotiations', or 'talks' with 'negotiations', or 'compromise' with 'bargaining'. In the context of industrial relations, the term collective bargaining is used to describe the process of management/ union negotiations. The parties may be negotiating, but they may not be bargaining. One of the aims of this book is to clear up some common misunderstandings about what these words mean. To understand better the process of negotiation we need to be more precise about our vocabulary.

The definitions given above, along with other commonly held ideas about negotiation, are not altogether wrong; their deficiency is that they are incomplete. They take a limited view of a complex process. Although compromise can be used in negotiation, for example, it is only one of several approaches.

Terms such as compromise, trading, conferring, bargaining, trade-off, conceding and so on are not synonymous with negotiating; they form part of the process. You can negotiate and reach agreement without compromising. Equally, two parties can trade without having to negotiate: they only need negotiate when they begin with divergent views/objectives.

Here is a workable definition of negotiation:

> *Negotiation is a process through which parties move from their initially divergent positions to a point where agreement may be reached.*

And parties move from their initially divergent positions usually in response to one or more of the following approaches:

- compromise
- bargaining
- coercion
- emotion
- logical reasoning.

The central point about negotiation is that it involves *movement*. Good negotiators know how to create that movement, choosing the right approach to take and the right point in the process to use it. Often they will use several approaches. Indeed, depending on the circumstances, they could conceivably employ all five approaches during the course of a negotiation. If a negotiation is successful it ultimately results in an agreement between parties.

1.3 Basic approaches to negotiation

Of the five basic approaches available, *compromise* and *bargaining* are the two used predominantly in both the UK and the United States. The British are known as great compromisers. Bargaining and compromise offer eminently reasonable approaches to negotiation. They can be described as 'legitimate' approaches because they always involve both parties moving towards each other's position.

Negotiating by using compromise or bargaining can be seen as a conciliatory way of doing business, as being fair and reasonable, as acting in a 'gentlemanly' fashion. Using these approaches, however, will often not give you the best deal.

Many British and American negotiators feel uncomfortable with using the more 'manipulative' approaches: *coercion, emotion* and *logical reasoning*. They prefer to stick to compromise and bargaining, often to their very considerable cost, particularly in international negotiations. Their counterparts in the Far East, the Soviet Union and in most southern European countries, however, are skilled practitioners at using emotion and coercion. The West Germans, meanwhile, are renowned in negotiating circles for their use of logical reasoning.

A full analysis of these five approaches is given in Chapter 2, but here is a brief introduction.

COMPROMISE

Compromise involves a search for the middle ground, a process through which parties make concessions until they arrive at an agreement. Compromise is typically characterized by statements like:

- 'Let's split the difference and meet in the middle.'
- 'Let's meet each other half way—50/50.'

In its favour, compromise is perhaps the quickest and simplest way to break a deadlock in a negotiation, particularly if the parties' positions are not too far apart. It is the least imaginative approach, however, and it could result in you conceding more to the other party than they would have been prepared to accept.

A compromise is made over a single issue: the salesperson wants a 5 per cent price increase and the buyer refuses—both parties move and agree to a 2.5 per cent increase. Compromise is often used by negotiators who are in a hurry. Research by the authors' consultancy group, Purchasing and Materials Management Services, shows that people are much more likely to compromise when they are face to face with the other party. No matter how hard-line your position may have been, personal contact with the other party can trigger a concession, a point we develop later in the book.

BARGAINING

Bargaining is where the parties to the negotiation trade options with each other. They give and they take, with each party making concessions. The key difference between bargaining and compromise is that bargaining will span a range of issues, and therefore the eventual agreement does not necessarily represent the mid-point between the parties' opening positions. Compromise, on the other hand, involves conceding on a single issue.

Obviously the more issues upon which the parties give and take, the more complex the negotiation: it becomes increasingly difficult to put a value on the worth of, say, two concessions where one concerns price and the other concerns after-sales service arrangements.

In summary, remember that the key point about bargaining and compromise is that both parties need to concede before the approach will work. The same condition need not apply, however, when negotiators use coercion, emotion and logical reasoning.

COERCION

Negotiators who are (or imagine they are) in a powerful position will sometimes seek to force the other party or parties into an agreement through coercion. Examples are where an employer gives a trade union leader an ultimatum: 'Either your members accept my pay offer, or I close the factory', or where a buyer threatens a salesperson, perhaps indirectly: 'You wouldn't want me to look for another source, would you?'

Some well-known large companies use their dominant market position to coerce their suppliers, their distributors, etc. If used correctly, it's a powerful negotiating approach. If it's misused, however, it can be counter-productive.

When negotiators are having little success moving another party through bargaining or through logical reasoning, they can get frustrated. And when they are frustrated, they may try to get their way by resorting to blunt threats or to bluffing about their intentions. Threatening or bluffing in the heat of a frustrated moment has obvious dangers: if someone successfully calls your bluff, you're in trouble. If successfully used, coercion usually leads to only one party conceding.

EMOTION

The role of emotion in negotiation is poorly understood in many Western countries. But a major determinant of negotiators' behaviour is how they feel towards the other party (warm or cold), how passionately or dispassionately they put their case or how they react to a negotiating ploy—with surprise, with anger, etc.

Of course we all hold certain views that may not be entirely founded on facts: prejudices which are emotional, not rational positions. Good negotiators use controlled emotion as part of their armoury, but should be wary of prejudice. Controlled emotion is characterized by statements such as:

- 'My boss will kill me if I accept . . .'
- 'I need your help to . . .'
- 'We can't afford that, what with . . .'

It is important when using emotion to make sure your body language is in tune with what you are saying. When a powerful emotional approach is used, it will often result in only one party conceding.

LOGICAL REASONING

We all like to consider ourselves reasonable people. It is hardly surprising then that we can easily be swung by a well-reasoned case. Negotiators use logical reasoning to support their position and, if possible, to undermine the other party's position. The more factual the case prepared, the more careful the research supporting a negotiator's position, then the greater is the likelihood that logic will win the day—unless, of course, the other party knows how to counter it.

A typical example is where a salesperson seeks a buyer's agreement to a price increase. The buyer, quite naturally but perhaps unwittingly, asks why he should accept it. If the seller can only offer a vague or very general explanation ('our costs have gone up'), then the buyer's negotiating position is strengthened. If, however, the seller presents a detailed, well-researched, logical justification for the increase, the buyer's position is weakened: he will feel/appear unreasonable to refuse.

If the logical reasoning approach succeeds, then usually one party will do all the conceding.

1.4 When is negotiation necessary?

Every day people discuss deals and reach agreements without negotiating. A discussion, a meeting, an interview are not the same as a negotiation. Sometimes parties will discuss their joint problems, will see that there is no real conflict, and will reach an agreement without either party having to move. They have reached a jointly acceptable agreement: they haven't negotiated.

Negotiation is necessary where two or more parties (who are in, or who could enter into, a relationship of some sort, e.g. political, business, personal) are faced with a difference of viewpoint or objective.

Because of this difference of viewpoint/objective, negotiation involves a fundamental component: movement. Without movement, negotiation will fail. Of course getting the other party or parties to move from their positions and towards yours is your objective. If you can't, either you move towards them, or the result is deadlock.

Before negotiation can begin, the parties involved need to feel that there is a possibility of an agreement beneficial to them emerging from the process. They will perceive that several different outcomes could result from the negotiation. And each party will usually recognize that its priorities may be very different to those of the other party/parties; indeed, they may rank in reverse order.

1.5 The ritual of negotiation

There is an element of ritual about the negotiation process. If a negotiation is too quick, for example, then at least one party is likely to feel dissatisfied. If you buy or sell something, and you haven't followed some of the basic steps of the ritual, you are likely to be unsure whether you have secured the best possible deal.

Imagine you're looking to buy a car, and you see the model you want advertised at, say, £4500. You look the car over, it's what you want, and so you make an offer. You offer the seller £4000 for it, and immediately he accepts your offer. He doesn't try to pull a higher offer out of you; he doesn't even pause to consider your offer. He just about snatches your hand off. How do you feel? You quite naturally feel that you could have bought the car for much less had your starting price been lower.

Imagine now that the same car has been advertised, that you have made the same offer—£4000—but this time the seller reacts differently. He says he won't accept your offer, but he is prepared to move. After a lengthy negotiation over the price, you and the seller eventually agree on £4100 for the car. How do you feel? Under these circumstances you feel you have worked for your concessions and have squeezed the best price out of the seller—even though you have ended up paying £100 more than in the first example.

A riddle:
You pay £4100 for a car and you're happy.
I pay £4000 for the same car and I'm unhappy.
How come?

The difference, of course, is that in the second example you've been through the ritual. Or at least you believe you have. It is conceivable that the other party has not really negotiated, but has instead simply talked through the ritual. Some of the points to watch out for to assure yourself that you are in a *real* negotiation are considered in a later chapter (Chapter 7).

Our research shows that directors and senior managers in many leading companies throughout the Western economies are consistently falling down in their negotiating. They are breaking the most basic rules of negotiation and are winning raw deals for themselves as a result.

1.6 Dealing with someone who won't negotiate with you

Research shows that when faced with a party who just refuses to move, the tendency is to give way—to make concession after concession in the misguided belief that if you keep moving, you will encourage a corresponding move from the other party. If you're not careful, you can continue moving your position until you have nothing left with which to trade. You are probably facing a very experienced negotiator who is manipulating you.

As we have already said, negotiation involves movement, and where manipulation is used, only one party may do the moving. Ideally, you should move very slowly from your initial position, for two reasons: first, because to move quickly serves to undermine the credibility of your original stance; and second, because once you begin to give, you must beware of a natural tendency to continue to hand out further concessions to prompt a response.

When you make your first concession to the other party, insist on something in return. If nothing is forthcoming, *do not* give again. Instead, try to adjourn the meeting.

1.7 When does negotiation actually begin?

The answer is: it can begin sooner than you think. This point is best illustrated with a real-world example. A couple of years ago, a Swedish engineering company fell victim to a wild fluctuation in currency values. Such was the appreciation of the Swedish krone in relation to sterling, that it needed to increase its prices to its UK customers by 35 per cent just to preserve its profit margins. Many companies would have given up. The situation seemed impossible!

> *Would you believe that a company could increase its prices by 35 per cent in a highly competitive market and still survive?*

We knew that with some careful negotiation, and some detailed planning work behind the scenes, it could be pulled off. In a nutshell the story went as follows: the company's first move was to look at its own costs, and having made all the savings it could, it still required a 20 per cent rise in its selling price into the UK market to preserve margins.

We prepared a detailed strategy. We had the sales manager telephone all his major customers in the UK to talk to their respective buyers about the 35 per cent movement in relative currency values. Using a prepared briefing, the sales manager talked around the subject, talked about some of the problems this created for his own company, and kept emphasizing the 35 per cent. Avoiding the temptation, he said nothing about increasing prices.

His next step was to take most of his big UK customers out to dinner. He took the opportunity to talk to them about the recent currency fluctuation, always referring to the 35 per cent movement.

Although the company had identified savings which between them meant that a 20 per cent price increase would maintain current margins, it decided to 'posture' at 24 per cent.

His UK customers were household name companies in highly competitive markets. Despite that, and in response to the sales manager's indirect approach, eleven of these companies contacted him saying they would accept a 35 per cent price increase. *This was before he had asked for an increase, and was well above what he planned to ask for.*

So some weeks after both the initial telephone call and the discussions over dinner, the sales manager wrote to his other customers requesting a 24 per cent price increase. A total of thirteen customers agreed to pay the 24 per cent increase, while some negotiated lower increases.

The net result was that the average increase achieved from more than 40 UK customers (most of which were among the country's top 100 ranking companies) was in excess of 25 per cent. As a consequence, the Swedish company *increased* its margins.

Negotiations can begin before we realize it—perhaps with a casual telephone call through which another party can indirectly implant an idea, conditioning our behaviour.

1.8 Why some negotiations fail

There are three common reasons why negotiations fail:

1 Because the views or the positions of the parties involved are simply irreconcilable. We have already discussed how negotiation involves movement by one or both parties. There is a spectrum through which parties move which can be characterized as follows: parties move from their *ideal* position through to what they see as a *realistic* position and then on to what they regard as their *fall-back* position, beyond which they cannot move.

Assume that there are two parties to a negotiation, A and B, both of

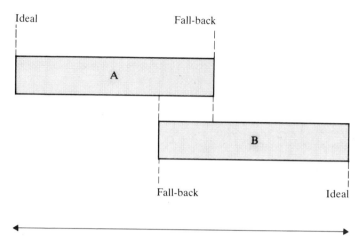

Fig. 1.1   The negotiating spectrum

whom, quite naturally, want to achieve an agreement most favourable to their interests. The simple diagram in Fig. 1.1 illustrates the room for movement available to A and B as they move from their ideal to their fall-back positions, at which point both would break off negotiations rather than move any further. From ideal to fall-back positions is the negotiating margin. A settlement is possible only where the two parties' positions overlap. If they didn't overlap, their positions would be irreconcilable.

In practice, of course, you will rarely have all the information you need to know precisely what your ideal and fall-back positions are. These positions may need to be assessed and modified as negotiations proceed and as you get a clearer picture of the other party's position.

2 Because of severe clashes of personality between the negotiators. A good example of clashing personalities came with the miners' strike in 1984: Ian MacGregor, head of British Coal at the time, was cool and logical, while Arthur Scargill, the National Union of Mineworkers' leader, was fiery and emotional.

3 Because a party to the negotiations is taken beyond his authority and so can move no further. It will sometimes become obvious during the early stages of negotiation that one or more of the parties will need to consult or introduce a more senior authority into the process. Until this is obtained the negotiation has to be adjourned or treated as a fact-finding exercise. (See section on defence in depth in Chapter 9.)

2

The five key approaches to negotiation

Having outlined the profile of negotiation, we will focus in this section on the five basic approaches that negotiators use to generate movement. To recap, negotiation is a process through which parties move from their initially divergent positions to a point where agreement may be reached.

The five approaches are:

- compromise
- bargaining
- coercion
- emotion
- logical reasoning.

To many people in the West, compromise and bargaining are seen as 'fair' means to reaching agreement. They see them as 'legitimate' approaches. On the other hand, coercion, emotion and logical reasoning, which are not so well understood in the UK and the USA, are regarded as underhand, or 'manipulative' approaches. This is an unfortunate attitude which can leave a negotiator working with one hand behind his back. This and other points are illustrated in several case studies below.

All five approaches are considered in turn here, together with some simple rules suggesting when and how each should be used.

2.1 Compromise

There are many things shared by English-speaking peoples, one of which is our propensity to compromise. That we commonly confuse the terms negotiate and compromise, seeing them as synonymous, is just a reflection of our view on the world. To us, agreements are reached by compromising. Are there any other ways?

Compromise is popular because it seems a 'fair' way to reach a settlement, because both parties move roughly equal amounts. A similar perception is held about bargaining—that it's a reasonable way to reach agreement.

The compromiser, who believes that agreement is to be found on the middle ground, uses plays like:

- 'Let's meet each other half way.'
- 'Let's split the difference between what I want and what you want.'

Your secretary wants a day off. But you've got so much work on you tell her it's impossible. You discuss the matter quickly and agree she will take a half-day. You have met in the middle, each getting exactly half of what you wanted. A compromise was, after all, the easiest way to reach agreement.

Compromising is quick and is often used to break a deadlock in a negotiation. It's unimaginative, however, and can result in you giving away more than you needed to, more than the other party would have been prepared to accept.

Compromise is different to bargaining. People compromise over a single issue, along a single dimension, whereas they bargain over several issues. When bargaining, negotiators give and take: a higher price for a quicker delivery; a discount for early settlement. Because of this single dimension, it is clearly easier to *value* concessions made during compromise.

Obviously then if two parties set out to find a compromise on one issue, the one that took the more extreme position is likely to come out on top (see Fig. 2.1). For example, if your secretary wanted a day off, she might be sufficiently astute to ask for two days off. That way she knows that when you meet her half way, she will get the day she wanted.

Rule one of compromise is: **Try to take an extreme but credible posture**. When the secretary asked for twice the time off she wanted, her posture was

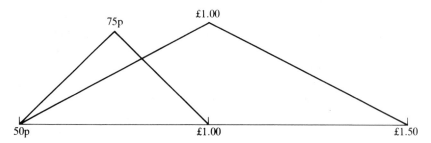

Fig. 2.1   If a buyer is offering 50p per widget, and the seller is asking £1, the compromise will fall around 75p. However, if the seller asks £1.50, the compromise will fall around £1

extreme, but it was still credible. Similarly, a buyer looking for a 5 per cent discount may be more likely to get it if he asked for 10 per cent than if he demanded his 5 per cent target.

Rule two of compromise: **Only use compromise as a last resort.** Try to find out more about the other party and to explore other approaches if possible. Imagine you are negotiating with someone you have not dealt with before. You have hardly begun and he suggests a compromise: 'Let's meet in the middle,' he says. You are then faced with several questions: Is he a poor negotiator? Is he short of time and using compromise to force a quick agreement? Has he taken an extreme position, knowing he will benefit most from compromising? You don't know the answer to these questions so you should decline his invitation to compromise.

Too many British negotiators use compromise as their first choice when it should be their last.

2.2   Bargaining

Most books on negotiating and most films on negotiating concentrate their attention on bargaining. Most American business people will 'bargain' with their customers/suppliers; the thrust of the US government's negotiating strategy was for many years based on bargaining.

Several years ago the US government entered into a particularly complex negotiation with a South East Asian government. It took place in Paris, but rather than hold sessions at their respective embassies, the parties decided to lease villas in the suburbs of the city.

The Americans took their villa for a fortnight which they assumed would be long enough. Being typically positive and somewhat impatient, the Americans hoped to clinch a deal within a week. After a fortnight they had got nowhere and had to renew the lease. During negotiations, the South East Asian party was extremely charming and attentive, but would not budge from their opening positions. The American party, anxious to make progress, began to give. And so it went on: the South East Asians remained extremely charming and thankful for each concession made by the other party; and the Americans gave way but got nothing in return. Every fortnight, the Americans renewed the lease on their villa.

After six weeks the American party was very frustrated. The South East Asians smiled but refused to move. Naturally, the Americans' frustration was vented from time to time in front of the other party (who remained charming and in complete control). They would shout and bang the table. And after every tantrum they would feel guilty and they would give further.

The negotiation went on for 19 months, throughout which the Americans continued to give without getting anything in return. In the end they had nothing left to give, while the South East Asians had still not budged. The US party's chief negotiator was later told that the South East Asians had taken out a three year lease on their villa!

Research shows that once a person has given, they are more likely to give again. Once they are moving, they are more likely to continue moving, determined that the other party will respond sooner or later.

Rule one of bargaining is: **Do not indicate that you are prepared to move quickly from your position.** While bargaining is about both parties moving, you will undermine the credibility of your own position if you move too soon. Should you do so the other party will dismiss your initial position either as extreme or without foundation. And once they have got you moving, you, rather than they, are most likely to make the next move. A common shortcoming of many negotiators is their predictability—don't get a reputation, for instance, of always taking a tough position but then consistently giving way on your demands. The opposition quickly pick up on your time-honoured tactics and will learn how to manipulate you.

Rule two of bargaining: **Move slowly, making the other party work for every concession they get.** The rule was illustrated in section 1.5 with the example of buying the car: when the buyer had to work hard for a concession it was seen as being more valuable. So the more slowly you move, the more value the other party may put on even a small concession.

Rule three of bargaining: **Avoid putting 'markers' down.** A marker is usually a figure—a price, a delivery period, a number of days holiday—which is your ideal position in any negotiation. By putting a marker down you immediately put a ceiling on what you can achieve, and you could prevent the other party from moving further in your favour.

Returning to the example of the car, suppose you have agreed terms with the dealer for buying the new car and the question then arises of a trade-in price for your old car. The dealer will probably ask you: 'What figure do you have in mind?' He wants you to put a marker down. While it isn't always easy, you should try to avoid giving the marker because you don't know what the dealer is willing to pay you for the car. If you give a marker and suggest you would accept, say, £3000, and that figure is within what the dealer was willing to pay, it won't be just accepted, but from then on the dealer will be under no pressure—the dealer can try to move your price downwards at no risk.

> *Avoid putting pressure on yourself.*

In this situation, you would be the only party under pressure. Experienced negotiators take care not to put pressure on themselves, but to apply it to the other party. Some ideas for avoiding putting down markers are given in the section on openings in Chapter 4.

Rule four of bargaining: **Get a return for any concession you make.** In the case above of the US negotiators it is clear that they continued to give in the hope that they would eventually draw a similar movement out of the South East Asian party. They didn't. With hindsight, it is easy to see how they fell into that trap. Many of us probably think it couldn't happen to us, but at home don't we sometimes find ourselves on the slippery concessions slope? You offer your kids £1 to cut the lawn and they refuse, so you immediately up your offer to £1.50, thereby breaking one of the simplest rules of negotiation. It is an easy trap to fall into.

So stay in control and avoid the temptation to continue moving. For any concession you make, ensure you get something in return before you consider moving again.

> *Avoid the slippery slope of granting one concession after another.*

Because bargaining involves give and take over a range of issues, the question of value inevitably arises. A price increase in return for an improvement in quality and a swifter delivery: is it a good deal? You should always try to emphasize to the other party the full value and benefits of any concession you make. On the other hand, you should play down and minimize the value and benefits of any concession they grant you.

Your success in bargaining will depend on winning greater value than you concede.

2.3   Coercion

Many leading European and American companies use coercion on their trading partners, in particular with their suppliers and their distributors, in the belief that by wielding their market muscle they will get what they ask for. Often they do. Yet what they ask for may not necessarily be the best deal going, and they may find themselves paying tomorrow for threats they make today.

Every single day big American and European corporations make bad deals by using their brawn more than their brains. We were recently involved in a typical case involving a leading British food retail chain where its clumsy approach and crude use of power eventually backfired. We cannot stress enough, however, that this is happening every day in the world of commerce. Obviously we can't reveal the name, so we've called the company XYZ Supermarkets.

XYZ Supermarkets Inc. demands that Real Fruits, its tinned fruit supplier, drops its prices by precisely 15 per cent, *or else*—or else, presumably, it will take its big business elsewhere.

It can't be denied that there are advantages to a dominant market position: it can help a buyer to get a better deal out of suppliers, but *only if it's used with great care.* Crude threats can be counter-productive. The XYZ Supermarkets buyer, by threatening to re-source, may secure the 15 per cent discount demanded. But ABC Stores, a leading competitor to XYZ Supermarkets, uses more subtle and more varied approaches in its negotiations with Real Fruits. It conducts its negotiations in a pleasant and respectful atmosphere. It uses approaches that support its position, including logical reasoning, perhaps about fruit market trends, and it uses bargaining techniques, perhaps in the form of offering to part-finance Real Fruits' future investment proposals.

As a result, ABC Stores secures an 18 per cent discount and slightly better payment terms for its tinned fruit supplies. And, should the tinned fruit market turn sour at some future date—if, for example, a dock strike creates a severe product shortage and supermarkets are clamouring for supplies— which of its customers is Real Fruits likely to help first? Quite naturally, the directors of Real Fruits would probably enjoy telling XYZ Supermarkets that it will have to pay substantially more if it's going to receive anything at all.

> *Use brains before brawn.*

In our seminars we have a short exercise which always creates substantial debate. We ask participants to draw a graph which illustrates the relationship between the *lowest* unit price which can be obtained for a particular item and the volume being purchased. Invariably participants draw a graph similar to Fig. 2.2 (a) which shows an inverse relationship between volume and price. This reflects what most people regard as a basic canon of commercial law: that the lower the quantity purchased, the higher the unit price.

While this curve is valid in illustrating the relationship between *average* unit price and volume, our research shows that the graph in Fig. 2.2. (b) more accurately reflects the relationship for *lowest* unit price. This is because first-

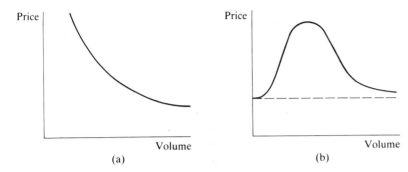

Fig. 2.2

class negotiators will often exploit particular commercial situations to obtain specially low prices for small volumes. Suppliers can be persuaded to make concessions for a small part of their sales which would be economically untenable for substantial quantities.

Another real-life example of threats backfiring happened with a food product in the 1970s, just prior to a sudden world shortage of the commodity. A leading Mexican businessman, who was a major supplier at the time, met with one of the largest buyers in the UK who marketed a well-known brand and who also sold on as a wholesaler to other retailers.

The Mexican met the buyer and told him that, due to rising costs, he would have to increase the price of his supplies from, say, $2 to $3 a kilo. The buyer said no, quite emphatically, insisting that he could buy all the supplies he wanted elsewhere at $2 a kilo. He told the Mexican supplier that unless the latter held his price to $2 a kilo he would lose the business. Attempts by the supplier to shave his price back to $2.90 a kilo led nowhere: the buyer insisted that $2 was his limit and repeated his threat to re-source from another supplier. He could, he said, get all he wanted elsewhere at $2 a kilo.

The Mexican supplier than asked if the buyer was still wholesaling supplies, and if so, at what price his company was selling on to retailers? The buyer said his company was still in that market and that the mark-up was 20 per cent. The Mexican asked if he could have an office and a telephone so he could ring his company. A little later he came back into the buyer's office with a written order which he handed to the buyer. It was an order—to buy a large amount from the buyer's company at $2.40 a kilo! The meeting ended abruptly with the buyer losing his temper and ordering the supplier out of his office.

The buyer then found that he couldn't buy elsewhere at $2 a kilo and that the market was moving quickly against him. He couldn't get adequate supplies to meet his company's needs and within three months supplies dried up entirely. Several months after their meeting, the Mexican businessman released supplies back onto the market—at $11 a kilo!

Rule one of using coercion is: **Before you threaten, think about the consequences.** Heavy-handed threats have a tendency to backfire on you, particularly when used against parties whose cooperation you may need at some point in the future. Even when closing one-off deals, such as buying an item of plant, remember that you may need to go back later for advice, servicing, etc. Negotiators are ordinary people who don't easily forget being threatened. Given the opportunity they will get their own back. So don't go over the top.

Rule two of using coercion is: **Use 'mirrored' or emotional threats rather than crude ones.** The mirrored threat is where you paint a scenario for the other party and ask what they would do if they were in your shoes. That way you leave it to them to utter the threat and then you agree. This technique is unlikely to leave the other party feeling resentful towards you.

The emotional threat is different, but just as subtle. It's typified by the comment: 'Don't force me to look elsewhere for this product.' You are saying that you don't want to re-source to another supplier, but if you have to it will be the other party's fault.

This 'kid-glove' technique was used to great effect by a lady purchasing manager within a Midlands engineering company. She had been instructed by her board of directors that for the third year running the company would be unable to accept any price increases from its suppliers. It was another zero-zero price freeze where she couldn't even balance one supplier's increase against a discount from another. There were to be no increases at all!

A castings supplier (let us call him AB Metals) telephoned her to say he was looking for a 9 per cent price increase. He felt his case was reasonable as the increase would only cover his own cost increases for the coming year and for the two previous two years. That was only 3 per cent a year, well below prevailing inflation.

The purchasing manager had been using AB Metals as a single source for castings for over two years, thereby getting a good price and enjoying low stock levels and just-in-time deliveries.

The purchasing manager told him there was absolutely no way she could accept any price increase this year. The supplier blew up and said he would stop deliveries the following month. She went to work on him: 'This puts me in a terrible quandary. We went into partnership with you a couple of years ago in an effort to improve our quality and our stock control and to improve your planning horizon. We knew there were risks when we agreed the deal.

Now I accept your view that a 9 per cent price rise over three years is perfectly reasonable. But you must understand that my board will not let me accept any price increases, full stop.

'I'll do what I can to help you in other ways—I'll try to increase volumes for you, I'll try to bring our payment dates forward. I'll try anything but I can't accept a price increase. What would you do in my shoes? I don't want to go elsewhere for supplies. Can you help me?'

While the purchasing manager retained her composure, the supplier became progressively more frustrated. She kept on asking him if he could help her solve her problem. Then the flustered supplier shot himself and AB Metals in the foot. He said he knew of another castings supplier in Glasgow which offered the same quality as AB Metals, which had compatible tooling, and which was consistently undercutting his company on price. He didn't stop there. He then told her about another supplier based in nearby Coventry which had recently bought all AB Metals' redundant machinery. It was knocking one-third off AB Metals' prices!

If you want to flex your market muscle in a negotiation, remember that the veiled or suggested threat is always more potent and has minimal consequences. Furthermore, if threats are to be introduced, they should be used well into the negotiation. A threat used early on will put the other party in the wrong frame of mind either to move or to help you.

2.4 Emotion

Emotion can be a very powerful approach in negotiation. After all, negotiators are not automatons. Indeed, if we examine many of the decisions we make, emotion plays a far larger part in them than we might care to admit. Like coercion, however, emotion has to be used carefully.

Take the security lock salesman who used to sell his wares by playing on a very basic emotion: fear. His patch was Lancashire where he would tour all the new housing estates door to door. He would ring a door bell, and when the home owner appeared, he would be standing upright in the doorway with a large hammer raised above his head. Once the poor occupant had got over the shock, he would explain that with the greatest of ease he could at any time gain entry to the house by breaking open the flimsy locks the house builder had fitted. The emotional impact of his pitch was such that on some estates as many as 80 per cent of householders bought security locks from him.

Emotion plays a large part in negotiations in Southern Europe, which is hardly surprising as it fits with the personalities of many Italians, Spaniards, Greeks, etc. In Japan and other Far Eastern countries, negotiators are often

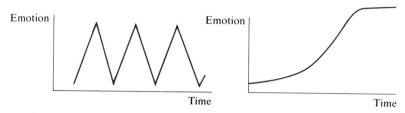

Fig. 2.3

expert at controlling their own emotions while knowing how to trigger—to their advantage—emotional reactions in you.

The two charts in Fig. 2.3 show different temperaments—which would you say reflected a Southern European, and which a British temperament? To make a very general statement, one could say that a Spaniard or Italian uses emotion constantly and will generally know how to bring it back under control. They flare up and cool down quickly. In contrast, it takes a great deal of provocation to upset the typical British person, and when the British do react it's when they are reaching boiling point. The tendency of the British to bottle up their emotions until they reach extreme proportions is a much-underestimated factor contributing to growing violence in British society.

The **only rule** about emotion is: **Control your emotions; don't let them control you.**

2.5 Logical reasoning

In contrast to the hot-blooded Southern Europeans, it is the cool, calculating Germans and Scandinavians who are the best exponents of logical reasoning in negotiation. When they present a case, say, for an increase in their prices, expect it to be backed by meticulous research, including a detailed breakdown of their costings.

This is where the buyer who asks the simple, reasonable question 'Why?' can land in trouble. For when the seller presents a reasoned, well-researched, detailed case backing such a position, the buyer can only resort to nit-picking. No one likes people nit-picking their case, particularly when they can answer queries quickly and factually. This is not to say that a buyer should not seek further information or should not challenge the other party's case—but it must be done carefully and with sensitivity as to how the other party is reacting.

Imagine the buyer has asked for logical reasons behind a price increase request and is given those reasons. Clearly the buyer will feel under pressure to accept the price increase, for to do otherwise would mean losing face through acting, apparently, irrationally. If the buyer then changes course and starts using emotive tactics like: 'Well anyway, we can't afford it,' it is clearly a defensive move and the seller will be justified in going 'cold' on the negotiation.

Rule one of logical reasoning: **Be careful how you use the *why* approach.** Most people resent their logical position being picked over: they become frustrated if others quibble over minor details.

> *Question, but don't nit-pick.*

If you anticipate that a forthcoming negotiation will be following a strictly logical course—where you're trading facts for facts—it makes sense to get your logic in first. If you can explain in adequate detail why your company could not possibly carry a price increase this year and hope to remain in business, and you get this logic in before the other party is able to provide a perfectly reasoned case for such a price rise, you have taken the negotiating 'high ground'. They then run the risk of 'nit-picking' your logic.

Rule two of logical reasoning, therefore: **Get your logic in first.**

Rule three of logical reasoning is: **Maintain the credibility of your logic.** If you are going to base your case on facts, make sure you've got them right and don't take the chance of assuming the other party won't check.

Several years ago, the authors were engaged in their consultancy capacity by one of Britain's leading pharmaceutical companies, which at the time was suffering a severe cashflow problem. After other sources of working capital had been explored and ruled out, the company (let us call them A1 Pharmaceuticals) decided its best option was to extend its trade credit. At the time, its average settlement period with its suppliers was 45 days. Its aim was to extend this to 70 days.

Most suppliers didn't even notice when A1 began paying its bills on a 70 day basis, and those that did accepted the extension. But around half a dozen initially refused to accept 70 day terms. We were brought into the negotiations with the reluctant suppliers and, within a couple of weeks, all but one company had agreed to the extension.

The very large supplier concerned (let us call it XYZ Chemicals) said it would allow A1 Pharmaceuticals an extension to 50 days only. This, according to its sales director, was his company's average debt collection period. We saw this as a clear signal of a substantial concession: if his average debt clearance period was 50 days, then some customers were probably paying in 60 days. In view of this, we advised our client that we could probably negotiate 60 day terms.

The board at A1 Pharmaceuticals was adamant, however, that every supplier would be paid on 70 day terms and no sooner, so we tried again. But we couldn't get XYZ Chemicals to move beyond 50 days and were told that XYZ would be stopping deliveries within ten days.

Then we decided to check the credibility of the sales director's case. We tracked down the accounts of the particular division of XYZ concerned and established that its average debt collection period wasn't 50 days, but was in fact slightly above 70 days.

We rang the sales director to tell him the good news: that A1's terms were within what his company was achieving. This prompted an angry outburst from XYZ's sales director who said that the accounts bore little relation to reality, that they were fabricated to satisfy the shareholders.

With the threat of delivery stoppage now looming, we wrote to the sales director, with a copy to his chairman, quoting what he had told us about the fabricated accounts. This was brinkmanship, but it worked. The chemical delivery arrived as usual the following week even though A1 had begun to settle its account on a 70 day basis, and deliveries continued thereafter unaffected. Two years later A1 was still receiving 70 days' credit from XYZ, even though it had reverted to 50 day terms with its other suppliers.

3

Short case studies 1

We believe it would be helpful at this point to consider how some of the principles, rules, etc., of negotiation can be applied in practice.

What follows is a set of nine typical negotiating scenarios each with multiple-choice answers. Work through these and make a note of your preferred option. At the end you will find what we consider to be the best course of action, together with reasons for the choice.

You can refer back to these when faced with similar situations in the future—try the option suggested and see if you get better results!

1 When do we begin?

You are a sales manager and you have been told by your management that it is necessary to achieve an average 20 per cent price increase on all sales in order to counteract currency exchange rates which have moved sharply against you. If you cannot achieve this, or close to it, your company will have to cease trading. The current inflation rate is 3 to 4 per cent per annum and most customers, if they needed to, could buy elsewhere within 3 or 4 months.

Would you:

(a) Ring up the buyers within your major customers and ask for a price increase?
(b) Send a letter to your customers requesting a price increase?
(c) Request a meeting with the buyers without specifying the reason?
(d) Invite them to lunch and then outline the problem?
(e) Do something else?

2 The challenging price increase

You have asked the buyer of a regular customer for a price increase of 4.8 per cent on a regular item. Current inflation is running at 5 per cent per annum.

What is the most effective remark that the buyer can now make and what is the best remark from a seller's point of view?

(a) 'No.'
(b) 'Why?'
(c) 'I was thinking of a decrease.'
(d) 'I can only afford half.'
(e) 'Can it be delayed?'

3 What do you do?

Your secretary has just informed you that one of your more important suppliers is on the telephone waiting to talk to you about a price increase for a range of manufactured components. Would you:

(a) Talk to him to ascertain his position.
(b) Invite him to come and see you to discuss the matter.
(c) Tell him you are not accepting any price increases.
(d) Pretend you are not in.
(e) Ask your secretary to request that he write to you with his company's point of view.
(f) Make comparisons with the movements of other suppliers.

4 Cash flowing the wrong way

Without any warning you receive a telephone call from a large customer informing you that it is going to lengthen its payment terms from 45 to 60 days. The buyer apologizes, but says that in the current climate there is no choice.

As the credit controller would you:

(a) Ask why the buyer is having to do this.
(b) Tell the buyer that you would then be being paid much later than your average debt collection period (even if this was not true).
(c) Tell the buyer that if this is insisted on you will have to stop delivery.
(d) Propose meeting half way at, say, 52 days.
(e) Invite the buyer to come and see you and make no comment on the phone.

5 Gentlemen

You are in a negotiation with someone you have never dealt with before. After a short introductory discussion, he suggests a compromise on the price, saying 'Let's split the difference—I'll meet you half way—a fifty-fifty split?'

If you accept this suggestion the price you will pay would be better than you had hoped for before the meeting. Do you:

(a) Accept.
(b) Decline.
(c) Tell him his offer is insulting.
(d) Make a counter offer which is a 10 per cent movement from your starting position.
(e) Stay silent.
(f) Explain that you are looking for more.
(g) Offer to give him something he wants if he reconsiders his position.

6 *Cash deal*

You are buying a car for cash. After some discussion with the salesperson you ask what discount is available for cash. The salesperson replies 'What did you have in mind?' Do you:

(a) Suggest a 5 per cent discount.
(b) Suggest a 10 per cent discount.
(c) Suggest a 20 per cent discount or more.
(d) Ask the salesperson again what the cash discount is.
(e) Ask for additional items to be included in the deal at no extra cost, e.g. radio, cassette player, mats, etc.

7 *Worth a million?*

You are negotiating to sell a million wine glasses and have offered them to the other party at 10p each. The buyer invites you in to consult and says 'Your price is not good enough.'

Which of the following actions would you now take:

(a) Cut your price marginally.
(b) Defend your price.
(c) Ask what other potential suppliers are offering.
(d) Ask what price the buyer has in mind.
(e) Say that your price is competitive and there is very little you can do.

8 *Brinkmanship*

You have been in negotiation for a long time and you are approaching an agreement. The other party is called out of the room by a telephone call, and when he comes back he abruptly announces that he will have to terminate the negotiation and can negotiate no further. He offers you a deal if you will accept the position already reached—take it or leave it. The terms are not particularly tough, but you are giving more than you had wanted to agree to. You hoped to get more. Which of these options would you choose, in answer to the ultimatum?

(a) Ask for a five minute recess with your people.
(b) Accept the deal.
(c) Pretend you didn't hear it.
(d) Ask for time to call your boss.
(e) Try to make him feel unreasonable.
(f) Decline.

9 A miserable offer

You are the buyer of a range of packaging items. You are in negotiation and your supplier has just surprised you with a $\frac{1}{2}$ per cent reduction on the price. Which of the following would you do?

(a) Tell him to increase it to 5 per cent.
(b) Ask him if he will increase it to 5 per cent if you give him a sizeable increase in business.
(c) Make a matching concession of your own.
(d) Take a sarcastic line and tell him how sensible he was to make it.
(e) Tell him it is nothing like enough.
(f) Thank him but insist he looks again to reduce the price further.

Answers

Case 1 answer: option (d) Negotiation can begin sooner than you may think! Refer back to the illustration given in section 1.7 of Chapter 1. You outline the problem over lunch, but do not ask for a price increase at that time—this is a seed-sowing exercise designed to 'condition' the buyer to expect a price increase at some time in the future. Alternatively, as we saw in the example of the Swedish engineering company (in the same section) you could begin the conditioning on the telephone.

Case 2 answer: For the buyer, the best remark is (c) This clearly indicates that getting the increase will not be easy and this may reduce the seller's expectations.

For the seller, (e) is the best alternative. This indicates that the buyer is probably prepared to pay since all that is asked for is delay. The way the question is put is very tentative and any objections can be overcome.

Option (b) could be very dangerous for a buyer. If 'why' is asked and a logical explanation is given, the buyer will be on the defensive—see section 2.5 in Chapter 2.

Case 3 answer: option (e)   The main purpose of the call is to canvass your reaction. By finding out how you react and what your position is likely to be, the other party can plan accordingly. By refusing to discuss the matter on the telephone, and instead asking the other party to write to you, you are putting the pressure on them. After you receive the letter setting out their position, you can plan how best to tackle the negotiation. The other party could be trying on the tactic successfully used by the Swedish engineering company in section 1.7. It is important to avoid being 'conditioned' by the other party, so be wary of option (b) inviting them to come in and discuss the matter: best to get their full position in writing before meeting eyeball to eyeball.

On the face of it, option (f) looks reasonable. Yet there is a danger of comparing one supplier's prices with its competitor because in practice companies often have entirely different cost structures from one another. If three suppliers offered you three different discount levels against identical starting prices you could be making a mistake by assuming the firm offering the biggest discount levels is the obvious choice. You may not be comparing apples with apples. The supplier offering the smallest discount may be a more efficient producer and you may be able to move them to offering the greatest discount.

Case 4 answer: option (e)   This reveals nothing of your position, and when the buyer is physically in front of you, some of the options may be used. You keep the customer guessing about your reaction. Better still could be to visit the buyer at his own premises. Option (c) would obviously be a somewhat crude use of power—it may succeed in the short run, but when the tables turn, as they surely will, you'll be in trouble.

Case 5 answer: option (e)   You have never met this person before and know nothing of his style in negotiation. If an offer is met with silence it is usually taken as rejection and an improved offer might be made. Option (c) would not be advisable—the other party has made a concession and if you dismiss it, they are unlikely to make further concessions. You should thank them for their move but tell them they must move further: it is important that the other party feels 'warm' towards you. Rejection will only turn them off.

Case 6 answer: option (d)   Avoid putting down a 'marker' too soon! This is what the seller is trying to get you to do—a valid tactic is to ignore the question and repeat your own. This forces the seller to put a 'marker' down. See section 4.2 in Chapter 4.

Case 7 answer: option (d)   As in Case 6, what you are trying to do is to get the buyer to put a 'marker' down. This is probably lower than the buyer is prepared to settle at and your negotiating skill should increase the figure closer to yours. Option (c) could be dangerous—the buyer might tell you other supplier's prices are lower. Option (e) would be alright if you stopped after the word 'competitive'. To say 'there is very little you can do' is to say you can do something—you're signalling a concession.

Case 8 answer: option (e)   People do not like to be thought unreasonable. It makes them feel uncomfortable. The approach 'It seems a pity to waste all the time we have so far spent', etc., might be appropriate. Using emotion is always a powerful approach. As an alternative you could use (a)—a recess could put the pressure on the other party (see Chapter 9).

Case 9 answer: option (f)   The other party has made a concession. He has moved towards you and your job is to keep him moving. By thanking him you take psychological possession of the concession, making it very difficult for him to withdraw it. Being sarcastic or dismissive is inappropriate for it could antagonize him and will at the very least make him 'cold' towards you. While being tough in negotiation, you should always be encouraging the other party to feel 'warm' towards you.

4

The phases of negotiation

The basic processes of negotiation can be undertaken in the space of a 30 second telephone conversation: the callers state their positions, one or both of them move, and then they reach agreement. Alternatively, the process can take years if the issues are complex and if each available phase of the process is carefully worked through, as is evidenced by the East–West arms reduction negotiations.

The four central phases of negotiation are: opening, testing, moving and agreeing. In this chapter, however, we will take a slightly broader view of the process, looking briefly at all the steps from preparation through to measuring your success:

- Preparation and planning
- Openings
- Testing
- Moving through making concessions
- Conclusions and agreement
- Measuring success.

4.1   Preparation and planning phase

What you do at this stage will determine the course and quite probably the outcome of the negotiation. Research shows that a key factor separating the skilled and the pedestrian negotiators is the way in which they prepare and plan their sessions. Of course those who say they have no time for any preparation or planning are most unlikely to be securing good deals for themselves or their companies. In the context of negotiation, preparation and planning have distinct meanings:

1 *Preparation* is concerned with researching the issues to be negotiated and is likely to include:
   (a) establishing the current state of the market, which may mean reading analysts' reports, talking to other companies, etc.;
   (b) understanding precisely what your own requirements are, which may involve meetings with colleagues;
   (c) researching the other party—perhaps a supplier or a customer—to find out what their strengths and weaknesses are, and to give you a feel for their ideal/realistic/fall-back positions;
   (d) deciding what your targets and your own negotiating spectrum is;
   (e) as well as researching facts about the other party, you will inevitably be making some assumptions—and it is important to identify and recognize the difference between the two.

2 *Planning* is where you look forward to the negotiation, imagine how the session will proceed and plan your strategy, much like an athlete plans a race strategy. Some of the questions you will try to answer here will be:
   (a) How will I open the negotiation?
   (b) How are they likely to respond?
   (c) How can I set the agenda?
   (d) How can I condition them and reduce their expectations?
   (e) If I'm negotiating in a team, what role will each team member play?
   (f) How will I respond to the difficult questions and issues the other party is likely to raise?

Both preparation and planning are important, but you will find that the most successful negotiators cut no corners on the planning stage: they visualize the meeting and plan how they will achieve their objectives.

Setting these objectives at the correct level is also crucial. Too high, and they will demotivate; too low, and they will be too easily achieved and seldom exceeded.

Our own research has shown how targets fundamentally affect the outcome. If you take a group of skilled negotiators and you set them a target of securing a 4 per cent price reduction in a negotiation, we have found that in the vast majority of cases they achieve it. Occasionally one or two creative negotiators win above 4 per cent, but most regard the target as the ceiling.

Contrast the skilled group with a group of unskilled negotiators and the outcome is interesting. Faced with the same circumstances but with a target of securing a 10 per cent price cut, the unskilled group will consistently achieve between 5 and 7 per cent. Of course as this is well below their target they can be initially disheartened, until, that is, they are told that they outperformed the experts. We have found that the higher the target, the more people achieve, provided the target is not so high as to demotivate a negotiator before negotiation even begins.

4.2 Opening phase

When two or more people meet to negotiate, the first thing they do *is not* to outline their companies' opening positions. They begin, of course, by greeting one another, exchange salutations, perhaps enquire of each other's health and the health of each other's businesses. If you know the other party well, you will be interested in their affairs. If you don't know them, you are at least being polite and civil.

If you choose to be impolite, to ignore the standard protocol, you will do yourself no favours. You will start the session with the other party feeling 'cold', when what you want is them feeling 'warm' towards you.

The start of this phase proper is usually marked by some form of position statement by each party. Their position statements will tend to be some distance from their true position to allow for movement towards agreement—you rarely get everything you ask for.

This opening position—well away from where you hope to settle—gives you time and space to negotiate for your target settlement. There is plenty of evidence to show that the more you ask for the more you get, for it reduces the expectations of the other party and helps to condition them towards making concessions.

However, the expected gains from an extreme opening must be weighed against the considerable loss of face that would result from a big climbdown to avoid a breakdown in the negotiation. The opening position must be credible. If you ask for a 20 per cent reduction in the price suggested and the most the other party can give is 5 per cent you will have to retreat from your position a very long way if you are to reach agreement, and your credibility will suffer accordingly.

To avoid this, your preparation should include a survey of the relevant market to enable you to take up a credible opening position. For example, if you are buying a house it is sensible to look at any similar properties for sale and see what the asking prices are. With a car, look around a number of dealers and see what sort of deals are on offer. In an industrial context you would obtain a number of quotations from a variety of suppliers and make sure their tenders were evaluated on an equal basis. Some suppliers may offer higher prices but include other benefits which should be given a monetary value before these comparisons are made.

Never accept a first offer, however attractive it may seem, because the convention is that you always demand more than you expect to get and offer less than you expect to give. If this is so then it must also be convention to reject the first and other early offers. If you ignore this opening convention and make your fall-back offer first, the other party is unlikely to do the same; instead they will reject what you propose and use that as the starting point from which to negotiate you down further.

Quick settlements should be avoided since they tend to result in extreme outcomes and therefore favour the more experienced negotiator.

The first position of either side has more effect on the final outcome than any of the later moves—subsequent negotiation will take place against the declared opening position. The skill comes in setting *your* opening position at the right level and responding to theirs in the right way. Specific figures should be avoided at this opening phase—do not put a firm marker down too early, though a certain amount of 'kite-flying' can be done.

For example, if you are pressed for a figure you can suggest one but describe it as a hypothetical figure. Suppose you think that in a particular case you would be lucky to get a 5 per cent reduction on the quoted price and the other party is pressing for a figure, you could reply that if they were prepared to drop 10 per cent you could sign the order then and there. There is no commitment at this stage—you are asking 'What if. . . ?' Do this fairly light-heartedly but watch for their reaction. Your proposal is almost certain to be rejected but you can then press *them* for a figure—the negotiating arena has then been outlined.

Another way of avoiding the marker is to deflect the question. If we go back to the car purchase example where you have a car to trade in as part of the purchase of a new one, when the question of its trade-in value arises, the seller will usually ask you 'What figure did you have in mind?' If you now put a figure on the table you will never get more than that and the seller will regard that as an opening position from which to try and negotiate you down.

One way of deflecting this question, and you should try to devise others, is to plead ignorance. Tell the seller that he is the expert in used car valuations since that is his job—he does it every day. Ask *him* to give *you* a figure. This is reasonable and puts the onus on him. His figure will be his opening position and is probably lower than he is prepared to settle at. You can then negotiate him up from this without revealing your own position.

At this opening phase of a negotiation you are usually operating on the basis of imperfect information and careful questioning is needed to remedy this. Open questions are used—the *who, why, how, when, where* types of questions—and you should listen carefully to the answers.

It is a good idea to write down the questions you want to ask. How many times have you come away from a negotiation and only later realized that you have not asked a vital question? If a question is avoided put a small tick against it to remind you to return to it later. If you press for an answer the other party may dig their toes in and refuse. By returning to it later you may catch them off-guard and get the answer you require.

> *Be persistent—don't easily accept*
> *no for an answer.*

4.3   Testing phase

At this phase each party promotes and explains its own position while probing the other's to search out weaknesses and areas where movement may be possible. Parties also test any assumptions which have been made during their preparation. In addition, one side will seek to influence the expectations of the other party and test the firmness with which they are likely to hold to their opening position. Assumptions should be written down prior to the negotiation to ensure each is tested for validity. Failure to do this could result in wasting time through having 'got the wrong end of the stick'. As each assumption is tested a tick or cross can be placed against it, according to whether it is correct or not.

Negotiable variables are also explored at this phase. These variables should also be written down to ensure all are properly investigated. The aim here is to see where movement may be possible and where the other party is likely to 'dig in'. Do not accept a 'no' at its face value—try asking the same question in a number of different ways. Only when you have received a constant 'no' should you accept it.

Using silence can be very productive when testing the other party. Silence can be uncomfortable, and so to break it they will talk—hopefully expanding on their position. A simple pro-forma can help here. List the variables in order of importance and tick or cross them as movement is indicated. This then focuses where you should concentrate your attention and what to avoid. Remember, if you dwell too long on the 'no' or crossed items you will run the risk of raising the emotional climate and move the other party away from you.

In order to succeed in this you should keep the other party talking along lines structured by you, and whilst there are a variety of tactics to use here, by far the most important are questioning and listening. Ask clear and unambiguous questions, listen to the answers, and note verbal and non-verbal signals, e.g. adjectives indicating strength of feeling and commitment (a little . . . extremely) and facial expression and posture which may indicate annoyance or discomfort.

If you are negotiating opposite a team, you can deliberately direct a question to a hitherto silent member to see if they will reveal something different or new.

You can delay indicating your position in a variety of ways such as:

- Indicate you do not find part of their case credible.
- Make a biased summary and see if they pick it up.
- Deliberately misunderstand something and see if they repeat the same explanation.
- State that you will respond but need some further clarification first.

Another objective during this testing phase is to influence the expectations of the other party—to condition them towards *your* point of view and to make them think that agreement with you will not be easily achieved. This can be done in a number of ways:

- Question the assumptions on which their position is based—remember it is rare that anyone has all the facts before a negotiation and assumptions have to be made. Try to anticipate the assumptions which the other party has made and how these may be challenged.
- Question the facts of their case. Acceptance of something as a fact depends on how it is perceived—show that your perception is different from theirs: the 'I don't see it that way' approach.
- Even if you accept the facts of their position, challenge the conclusions which they have drawn, using statements such as 'But that could also mean. . .'.
- Look for inconsistencies in a complex posture. This requires very careful listening if you are to pick up any omissions. The chances of inconsistencies occurring are increased if you ask them to repeat the point—the 'I would be grateful if you could talk me through that again' approach. Again, this must be done with great care so as not to cause any ill-feeling.
- Make direct or indirect suggestions that they need to revise their position—use such approaches as 'How would that sound to you if you were sitting where I am?' It is essential both to listen and observe in order to note reactions and signals of where attitudes may be changing—where doubt is beginning to emerge in the strength of their belief in their case.
- Try to get them worried about the credibility of their position. Question age, experience, qualifications, authority level, etc. The other party's authority should always be established early in any negotiation and this can be done very easily by a question such as 'If we reach agreement now, can you decide for your organization?' You need to be sure you are talking to the right person. It also prevents them from drawing out your case and

then postponing the decision by stating that it will need further consideration.

- The other party will have prepared for the negotiation on the basis of information you have supplied them. In buying a car you will probably indicate that you are looking at a particular model for certain reasons. In buying a house you will indicate certain criteria which have led you to look at that type of property. In an industrial buying situation you will probably have sent out an enquiry document. At this testing stage you can introduce new information which forces the other party to make a readjustment to their prepared case. They may then indicate an extent of movement greater than you thought because they have not had time to think it through. If looking for a car, you may indicate that the estate version is perhaps the one you need, or you could say the children are of an age where they will be leaving home soon and you will not need the room. A components buyer could say that since sending out the enquiry he now finds he could order more. If the other party is keen to do a deal they may indicate that they could do far more than you at first thought.
- Present your case well, emphasizing strengths and minimizing weaknesses, demonstrating mastery of detail, and stressing the benefits that will accrue to the other party should they accept the deal offered.

4.4 Moving through making concessions

In this phase of a negotiation you try to get the maximum amount of movement from the other party from their original position, while making the minimum movement from your own. Movement can be encouraged in a number of ways:

- *A progressive and supportive summary*, which highlights areas for possible movement. This should be done with enthusiasm—if it appears that you lack conviction that movement is possible, it is highly unlikely that you will get it!
- *Joint departure*—proposing that *both* parties revise their original positions or refer back for consultation, though this should be used carefully. As an illustration one might propose: 'I think we could look at the quantity we are ordering and you could look at the price you are offering.'
- *Hypothetical linked concessions*, where the 'If you . . . then I' approach is used. Hypothetical proposals are very useful since they can provide a way out of deadlock and also enable new ideas to be put forward free of any commitment. However, you need to be careful in making hypothetical proposals that you do not give away too much of your thinking and reveal your position.

- *Issues can be linked together* as a way of getting movement. It should be used tentatively—'Do you think there is anything to be gained from looking at A and B together?'
- *Emphasize what you have conceded*—you usually have to make concessions and, having done so, you can appeal to the other party to accept what you have done in an effort to get them to go further.
- You can also *appeal to the good nature of the other party.* This is essentially an emotional, persuasive stance but can be very effective, especially when linked with humour.
- *Putting on pressure.* This can be done in a number of ways: using time deadlines, introducing coercion by competitive pressures, or by making an emotional plea for help.

Encourage the other party to move and then try to keep them moving. If you can do this you might be able to increase the momentum and obtain even more. However, be careful that you do not get so caught up in the process that *you* concede more than you originally intended!

CONCESSIONS

A concession is a revision of a previous position you have held and justified publicly. Concessions are necessary to reach agreement, but the parties nevertheless try to move as little as possible. Negotiators usually work on the assumption that the other party knows and will follow the 'must move' convention. The skilled negotiator is always prepared to remind the other party of this, either to exert pressure or to point out that he is not 'playing the game'.

Always try to promote in the other party a willingness to make concession by:

- convincing them that they cannot hold to their present position;
- showing them how they can move without loss of face—never 'paint them into a corner';
- indicating that you too will move at some time. A good concession is a small one—major shifts make it difficult for the negotiator to maintain a credible position and will almost certainly encourage further pressure from the other party to move even more!

Concessions offered without specific pressure being applied are not worth much. They should be accepted, as should *any* concession, but only as a stepping stone towards others. You may sometimes be in a position where you have little or no room to manoeuvre, but generally it is courting disaster to go into any negotiation with no concession in mind or possible.

Any concession presents you with three problems:

1 Should I make it now?

We have already stated that major concessions, made too soon, only encourage the other party to press for more without necessarily making any themselves. On the other hand, you are unlikely to induce a willingness to move on the part of the other party if you appear stubborn and obdurate. Try, therefore, to make a concession on some very minor straw issue sufficient to show that movement is possible without in any way giving the impression that you will be a pushover. If the other party makes a concession it is probably up to you to make one also. This helps the process and maintains the 'warm' climate between you.

2 How much ground should I give?

In section 2.2 in Chapter 2 concerning rules for bargaining, we advocated moving slowly and in small increments. This goes a long way to answering the problem posed here. The concession you make need not match one offered to you but must not be disproportionately small—you will then appear unreasonable. Always value any concession you make in the other party's eyes—something you can easily give may be of real value to them!

3 What am I going to get in return?

Concessions are 'traded' and should not be made without return. As said above, value any concession you make not in *your* terms but in those of the other party. You can then better judge what you ought to get in return, and propose withdrawing the concession if the 'trade' appears unbalanced.

Buyers should beware of 'packaged' concessions where a number of items are brought together and a 'collective' concession offered. Sellers, of course, should try to package, making concessions appear more appealing: the 'If you will do X, Y and Z then I will offer A' approach. A buyer should value the X, Y and Z separately and make sure that their sum equates to A.

Try to make a *small* concession from you look like a major concession to the other party; you can then expect a correspondingly *real* major concession from the other side. These are what are called 'straw' issues. Identify such issues on *your* side but also try to anticipate those which the other side may use so that you do not trade real substance for a minor return.

Responding to concessions can be a problem. Low responders tend to be the most successful negotiators and it is difficult to deal with them because they offer restricted information, verbal and non-verbal, for you to assess progress. They reduce the risk of making quick answers and maintain pressure through their 'low profile' approach. It is not necessarily the 'only style', but some of its strengths should be noted and built into your style if possible.

In summary, be prepared to give ground but do so slowly and try to get the other party to move first. Keep concessions small and try to make fewer than the other party. Always look for something in return for every move you think of making.

> *Thank people for*
> *any concessions—no matter how small.*

" MR. HODGES, IF I AGREE To BREAK FOR COFFEE AT 10·30 AM, WILL YOU COME DOWN ANOTHER £10,000 ON THE INSTALLATION COSTS, BRING FORWARD DELIVERY To JUNE AND ALLOW US 90 DAYS To PAY ? "

A MINOR ISSUE IS MADE To LOOK LIKE A MAJOR CONCESSION

4.5 Conclusions and agreement

A common problem is to try to answer the question 'When is a negotiation approaching a conclusion?' It is difficult to give a definitive answer but a number of pointers can be identified:

1   The repeated 'no'

A single 'no' should rarely if ever be taken at face value. One skill the successful negotiator must develop is the ability to ask the same question in a variety of ways. If, having tried this, the answer is still no, the subject should be put to one side—further pressure will only raise the emotional climate with possible detrimental results.

2   Concessions get progressively smaller

Fine judgement is necessary here because, while concessions are always worthwhile, you can demand too much. A sure sign you are reaching the limit is when concessions become smaller and smaller. Depending on circumstances the skilled negotiator must decide when to stop. In a 'one-off' purchase situation, you can push to the limit of the repeated 'no'. Where future continuous dealing may be necessary it may be wise to take a longer term view and stop before this stage is reached. There is always another day!

3   Signals

As has been stated earlier, body language can be difficult to control as it is ingrained in you. Non-verbal signals can indicate when the other party has moved as far as they are prepared to. Some of these are:

- *Shuffling*—an active pattern of behaviour not previously shown.
- *Sweating*—another uncontrollable aspect of behaviour.
- *Colouring up*—another sign of stress which shows a limit is being reached.
- *Faster breathing*—a common symptom of excitement or anticipation of a conclusion being close.
- *Pen put down/papers or files closed*—care is needed in interpreting such signals. Because they are so obvious, many negotiators do this deliberately to convey a message. It is not easy to determine whether the message is genuine or it is just being done for effect.
- *Eye contact*—when two people have each other's attention they look at one another. It follows, therefore, that when attention declines so does the extent of eye contact.
- *Tone of voice*—excitement raises the tone of voice and disinterest lowers it. Verbal behaviour can indicate internal feelings—a lowering of the normal tone of voice can indicate a preparedness to withdraw, often before the intention has been fully formed.

These are some indicators that a negotiation may be drawing to an end. However, we should carefully observe those with whom we negotiate on a regular basis so that we can understand their behaviour and what it means.

As the negotiation moves towards a close we begin to enter the 'final offers' arena. When a final offer is announced it should be treated with the same reservation and caution as opening demands. Research studies have shown that rarely is either side pushed to its absolute limits—the art is to convince the other party that they cannot push you any further. They may accept this if:

1 Your final offer is tabled with conviction—a simple statement free from any form of qualification is more effective than one backed by a mass of reasons. The more reasons you use to back a position, the more it appears that you are trying to convince yourself and the less the effect on the person you are negotiating with.
2 Your final offer is not seen as yet another in a chain of final offers. This problem is often seen in labour relations negotiations where management make a succession of so-called final offers.
3 Your previous preparedness to move, albeit small and slow, is no longer apparent despite pressure that may be applied.
4 Your non-verbal behaviour, some aspects of which have been outlined above, is in line with your verbal behaviour. If this is not the case you will appear insincere and will not be believed.

The aim during the conclusions is to finalize an agreement which will be implemented in the manner in which it was intended. It must also be recognized that agreement may not result from negotiation. Merely because we enter into a negotiation does not necessitate agreement and we should be prepared to break off negotiations if it becomes clear that there is no prospect of a result with which we can agree. In this event we may decide to end the contact and adjourn or postpone any further discussion for a time to allow for reappraisal.

Given that a negotiation appears to be moving towards an agreement, a number of important guidelines apply:

1 If you do make a final offer this should be done with conviction and free from any form of qualification. A simple statement 'This is my final offer—take it or leave it' or 'This is my final offer—here is my cheque' involve a qualification of the offer and could either annoy the other party or give them hope that you can be made to go further. Never let it appear that your final offer is merely one in a chain of final offers.
2 It is possible to realize when a negotiation is approaching a conclusion—concessions get smaller and smaller and despite pressure being applied there is no longer a willingness to move or make alternative proposals. Whilst such alternative proposals are being made you are almost certainly still in the moving phase of the negotiation.

3 Deadlock can often appear to have been reached but beware that this is not being used deliberately to extract some final concession. In such situations it is common for deadlock to be broken by the other party proposing a compromise—a 'let's split the difference' approach. Remembering the rules for compromise outlined earlier, try to ensure that such a compromise is not to your disadvantage.

4 Consider the use of 'closing' techniques in order to push an uncertain negotiator that final distance which will lead to an agreement. Sellers use such techniques but buyers less so. An order already written out and merely needing the buyer's signature, the open cheque book, the outstretched hand ready to shake on the deal can be powerful persuaders.

5 Finally, make absolutely sure that you know what has been agreed—too often one or other party to an agreement is surprised when the confirmatory letter arrives containing items to which they do not remember agreeing. Clear, concise summaries are essential at this phase of a negotiation. 'Closed' questions requiring unambiguous yes/no answers should be used and careful notes taken of the answers.

If a confirmatory letter is necessary then this should be drafted as soon as the negotiation has finished and sent to the other party as soon as possible.

> *The memory plays tricks.*

The longer that written confirmation is delayed, the greater the chance of uncertainty over whether you agreed or not to some often relatively insignificant point, but one which just gives that little bit extra to the other party.

4.6 Summary—the phases of a negotiation

Subsequent analysis will show that virtually all negotiations progress through the above phases. However, there is no sudden transition from phase to phase—they tend to merge into each other. The skilled negotiator needs to be aware of when the transition takes place and behave accordingly.

An observed criticism of many negotiators is that they move too quickly from the testing phase to the moving phase—they do not test fully to see just what possible movement there might be. All variables should be *fully* explored for potential movement before any actual moving proposals are made.

One important stage in the negotiation process which must not be overlooked is measuring your performance. Only by measuring your successes and failures can you: first, assess your progress as a negotiator; second, determine precisely what you achieved out of the negotiation; and third, learn from any mistakes made this time which need not be repeated next time.

4.7 Measuring success

In Chapter 1 it was stated that agreement was reached in a negotiation when the *perceived* value to each party was seen to be acceptable. Perception is very much a subjective area, however. Two different people faced with the same negotiation may judge success very differently. If an acceptable result has been obtained then as far as the parties involved are concerned the negotiation has been successful.

Care is needed, however, to ensure that the desire for a successful outcome does not mean that targets are set too low. The skilled negotiator is constantly seeking to improve—to be more successful. It is rare that you will leave a negotiation feeling that if it were to be done again nothing would be changed—there is nearly always some opportunity which is perceived after the event when it is too late to do anything about it. This need not be demotivating, and it can be turned into a positive force. One way of doing this is, as part of the post-negotiation review, to write down a short summary of what went well and what went not so well.

Put your notes away in a drawer and after three or four negotiations take them out and study them. Look especially for items which recur in the 'Went not so well' column—these are weaknesses on which work is needed.

4.8 Central phases of negotiation—checklist

THE OPENING PHASE
Purpose:

- To establish a relationship and set the scene
- To take control . . . sensitively/assertively
- To communicate own expectations and to begin conditioning the expectations of the other party.

'Opening phase' issues to deal with during planning are:

1 Decide type of opening and opening statements to be used.
2 Identify 'common ground' issues which can usefully be mentioned to ensure that the negotiators present at least start together (e.g. agree purpose; recap on previous discussions; common problems/opportunities).
3 Decide how to phrase the requirement for the goods or services needed . . . saying enough to start the discussion but not to reveal your total hand. Write a point-by-point summary to refer to.

4 Plan credible and realistic comments about your own needs, and credible but 'diminishing' comments about the seller's claim or position.
5 Decide tactics for obtaining and keeping control.

TESTING PHASE
Purpose:

- To obtain information from supplier and to test own assumptions
- To assess the level of the supplier's interest
- To test how firm the supplier is on key points
- To probe for weaknesses in the other's arguments and to diminish confidence in them
- To 'fly kites' and observe response.

'Testing phase' issues to deal with during planning are:

1 Predict supplier's questions and arguments and decide how they will be answered or defused.
2 Phrase 'open' questions to test own assumptions and to encourage free flowing information-giving from supplier.
3 Anticipate the reasoning which the supplier will use to support his/her position and gather facts and arguments to undermine it.
4 Plan how to find out the supplier's 'shopping list' and how to avoid revealing one's own.
5 Anticipate which persuasion mechanisms will be used by supplier and prepare to match them.

MOVING PHASE
Purpose:

- To persuade the supplier to move as far as possible towards agreeing with the buyer's view on a particular subject, recognizing that the buyer may have to concede some ground on this, or another point
- To control the extent to which the buyer moves away from the ideal settlement point, and to know what this means in terms of the total cost of doing business.

'Moving phase' issues to deal with during planning are:

1 Work out the cost of concessions for each negotiating variable, and also estimate what the costs to the supplier might be.
2 Decide the 'concession increments'.
3 Decide what concession trade-offs will be cheap to you but which will be valued by the supplier.

4 Assess what personal or corporate needs the supplier has which the buyer, or the deal, may be able to satisfy.

5 Plan how the supplier can concede without losing face.

6 Make plans for overcoming deadlock . . . and adjournments.

7 Plan responses to any 'dirty tricks' which may be played.

AGREEING PHASE

Purpose:

- To reach workable agreement on the negotiated issues
- To agree next steps
- To keep control of what has been agreed
- To set scene for ensuing working relationship
- To gather information . . . for next time!

'Agreeing phase' issues to deal with during planning are:

1 Prepare 'closing tactics' and other actions which will help to establish common ground agreement.

2 Decide how to obtain supplier's confirmation of the points agreed and for the buyer to retain control of the summarizing/recording process.

3 Prepare proposals for next steps to 'keep talking' if agreement has not been reached.

4 Assess what information the supplier may reveal during 'post-agreement relaxation' which he is not prepared to divulge during the earlier phases.

5

Building a profile of yourself

As you set about improving your negotiating, you will find it invaluable to build a picture of yourself which identifies your strengths and weaknesses and which will monitor your gradual changes in behaviour and attitudes.

The questionnaire that follows is designed to help you improve your understanding of the process and to profile yourself as a negotiator. Answer each question as quickly and as honestly as you can by circling the number (between 1 and 7) which equates with your feelings. You are offered two statements in answer to each question and these appear on either side of the 1 to 7 scale. So if you strongly agree with the left-hand statement, then answer 1. If you feel less strongly, answer 2, etc. And obviously if you strongly support the right-hand statement, then circle 7.

There may be instances where you agree with both of the statements offered; if so, circle 4.

When you have completed the questionnaire, turn to the scores given in section 5.2 and calculate your total by adding up all the positives and subtracting all the negatives. In this section we also give model answers and explain why we score your answers as we do.

5.1 Questionnaire

1 How do you regard the process of negotiating?

Very competitive | 1 | 2 | 3 | 4 | 5 | 6 | 7 | Cooperative

2 Do you go into a negotiation looking for:

A fair deal | 1 | 2 | 3 | 4 | 5 | 6 | 7 | Or to win?

3 What result do you aim for?

A good result for your company | 1 | 2 | 3 | 4 | 5 | 6 | 7 | A good result for both parties

4 Before negotiating do you try to ascertain the authority vested in the person representing the other party:

Always | 1 | 2 | 3 | 4 | 5 | 6 | 7 | Never?

5 Before negotiating do you try to assess the other party's position:

The position of him/her personally | 1 | 2 | 3 | 4 | 5 | 6 | 7 | The position of the organization?

6 If you consider the personal position of the other party, does this evoke sympathy for the problems he/she is facing?

Never | 1 | 2 | 3 | 4 | 5 | 6 | 7 | Usually

7 In relation to question 6, does this affect your targets/objectives?

Usually | 1 | 2 | 3 | 4 | 5 | 6 | 7 | Never

8 How important are clear targets/objectives for negotiation?

Fairly | 1 | 2 | 3 | 4 | 5 | 6 | 7 | Very

9 When you move towards the other party's position in a negotiation, do you:

Move extremely slowly | 1 | 2 | 3 | 4 | 5 | 6 | 7 | Concede quickly?

10 Do you ever lose sight of the targets you set for a negotiation?

Rarely | 1 | 2 | 3 | 4 | 5 | 6 | 7 | Always

11 If you are in a meeting and you don't understand something, do you:

Usually let the matter pass | 1 | 2 | 3 | 4 | 5 | 6 | 7 | Always ask a question?

12 When you negotiate how committed are you to the objectives/targets set for the negotiation?

Totally committed | 1 | 2 | 3 | 4 | 5 | 6 | 7 | Fairly committed

13 When somebody says 'economy size' do you imagine something:

Large | 1 | 2 | 3 | 4 | 5 | 6 | 7 | Small?

14 Do you consider that a skilled negotiator should be satisfied at the outcome of a negotiation:

Rarely | 1 | 2 | 3 | 4 | 5 | 6 | 7 | Frequently?

15 How important do you feel power is in determining the outcome of a negotiation?

Very important | 1 | 2 | 3 | 4 | 5 | 6 | 7 | One of many important factors

16 How important is product knowledge in a buying/selling negotiation?

One of many important factors | 1 | 2 | 3 | 4 | 5 | 6 | 7 | The most important factor

17 Assumptions are frequently made prior to a negotiation. Do you ever write them down and check their validity afterwards?

Always	1	2	3	4	5	6	7	Never

18 During contact with other people do you usually:

Control your emotions

1	2	3	4	5	6	7

Allow emotions to control you?

19 Do you ever answer your own questions?

Often	1	2	3	4	5	6	7	Never

20 How important is individual initiative in negotiation?

Very	1	2	3	4	5	6	7	Not at all

21 Which do you do more in negotiation:

Listen	1	2	3	4	5	6	7	Talk?

22 Which do you pay most attention to during preparation for a negotiation:

The other party's weaknesses

1	2	3	4	5	6	7

The other party's strengths?

23 Which do you pay most attention to during preparation for a negotiation:

Your strengths

1	2	3	4	5	6	7

Your weaknesses?

24 If someone misunderstands a communication from you, who do you assume is at fault?

You | 1 | 2 | 3 | 4 | 5 | 6 | 7 | Them

25 Does your concentration wander during business meetings?

Rarely | 1 | 2 | 3 | 4 | 5 | 6 | 7 | Often

26 Do you stick to your plans in a negotiation?

Rarely | 1 | 2 | 3 | 4 | 5 | 6 | 7 | Always

27 When do you deal with the most controversial or important issues in a negotiation?

In the early stages | 1 | 2 | 3 | 4 | 5 | 6 | 7 | Later on

28 Do you feel happier negotiating:

On your own premises | 1 | 2 | 3 | 4 | 5 | 6 | 7 | On the other party's premises?

29 How do you feel about making a very low offer when you buy something?

Terrible | 1 | 2 | 3 | 4 | 5 | 6 | 7 | Comfortable

30 How do you feel when with people who hold higher positions?

Uncomfortable | 1 | 2 | 3 | 4 | 5 | 6 | 7 | Very comfortable

31 How do you feel when you meet someone who talks too much?

Indifferent | 1 | 2 | 3 | 4 | 5 | 6 | 7 | Annoyed

32 How do you feel when someone congratulates you on a job well done?

Flattered

1	2	3	4	5	6	7

Indifferent

33 How do you feel when someone says 'no' to you in a dogmatic way?

It will be very difficult to overcome

1	2	3	4	5	6	7

It will not be too difficult to overcome

34 Do you concentrate upon gauging people's feelings as well as getting the facts?

Often

1	2	3	4	5	6	7

Never

35 Do you readily admit to mistakes when they occur?

Often

1	2	3	4	5	6	7

Never

36 Do you generate new ideas in a negotiation?

Rarely

1	2	3	4	5	6	7

Always

37 Do you ever ask several questions at the same time?

Rarely

1	2	3	4	5	6	7

Often

5.2 Model answers

Some points to remember:

• Having completed the questionnaire you can now assess your negotiating profile by comparing your answers with ours.
• Go back to those questions where you scored 0 or negative and think about the answer we have given and why we have given it. These scores reveal some weaknesses in your approach and need working on.

- Where you have scored + 8 or + 10 on a question, these are your strengths which you should play to and build upon.
- Go through the questionnaire regularly (once every 6 or 12 months) to see how you are improving.

The scores shown below—positive, negative and zero—relate to points on the scale for each question.

1

	1	2	3	4	5	6	7
	+ 10	+ 8	+ 6	+ 2	0	− 2	− 4

Remember trained negotiators are out to get the best deal they can, and will work to get this. If you set out to cooperate you will blunt your competitive edge, though cooperation may be necessary *in the end*!

2

− 4	− 2	0	+ 2	+ 6	+ 8	+ 10

Look after *your* interests and let the other party look after theirs. It can happen that in trying to be fair you move too far towards the other party. Our perception of fairness could be incorrect—see question 13.

3

+ 10	+ 8	+ 6	+ 2	0	− 2	− 4

If you got + 10 on Question 2 you should have + 10 here! You must *always* have your company interests at heart—*remember* that is what you are paid to do!

4

+ 10	+ 8	+ 4	0	− 2	− 4	− 6

It is important to know this, since you may find yourself having declared your hand, only to find the other party cannot make the decision. As a matter of priority, ask if they can commit their company if a decision is reached.

5

−− 2	0	+ 8	+ 10	+ 8	0	− 2

You want as much information as you can get about the person and the company. Where the company stands in the market, whether it is part of a group, its financial status, etc., is all vital information.

6

+ 10	+ 8	+ 6	+ 2	0	− 2	− 4

It may sound a bit heartless, but sympathy for the other person may lead to you making concessions or not obtaining the best deal for your company.

7

− 4	− 2	0	+ 2	+ 6	+ 8	+ 10

This ties in with the *never* in question 6. Sympathy, for the skilled negotiator, does not deflect him or her from the achievement of objectives.

8

− 4	− 2	0	+ 2	+ 6	+ 8	+ 10

As with any situation, if you don't know where you're going any road will take you there! Know what you want and go out and get it! Don't try to make up targets and objectives as you go along—too many negotiators try to do this with poor results.

9

+ 10	+ 8	+ 6	0	− 2	− 4	− 6

If you move easily and quickly, you will be seen as a 'soft touch'. Move slowly and make the other party work for every movement you make. *Remember*—never make a concession without getting something back for it!

10

+ 10	+ 8	+ 6	0	− 2	− 4	− 6

It is easier to lose sight of targets set for a negotiation than most people think. Our research shows that sometimes as many as 80 per cent can lose sight of their objectives in a simulated negotiation.

11

− 6	− 4	− 2	0	+ 6	+ 8	+ 10

How many times have you been grateful to someone for asking a question at a meeting when you have thought you would look silly if you asked it! Asking if you do not understand something is strength *not* weakness, removes misunderstanding, and saves time.

12

+10	+8	+6	0	−2	−4	−6

Commitment leads to conviction. If you are convinced of your case you will push harder to get it.

13

−4	0	+8	+10	+8	0	−4

This question is all about perception. This can affect our objectives and measurement of success, to name just two—an economy *car* is *small*, an economy pack of, say, soap powder is *large*. It all depends on the context in which the word is used.

14

+10	+8	+6	0	−2	−4	−6

The skilled negotiator will analyse negotiations after the event to see what can be learned. In most cases some missed opportunities can be found. He is always seeking to improve.

15

−4	−2	0	+4	+6	+8	+10

Power is clearly important, but regarding it as very important can lead to an over-reliance on power to the neglect of other means of achieving what you want. Use of power is usually resented by the other party, making them reluctant to move. People remember with bitterness the use of crude threats and you may suffer later if the balance of power moves against you!

16

+10	+8	+6	+2	0	−2	−4

It has been demonstrated that product knowledge, whilst important, is only one factor in negotiation. Sufficient product knowledge can be grafted on to buying skill more easily than visa versa. Detailed product knowledge can lead to an over-concentration on technical aspects and obscure the real purpose of the negotiation.

17

+10	+8	+6	+2	0	−2	−4

This emphasizes the importance of planning. The best way to ensure that assumptions, which have to be made, are checked is to do it methodically—write them down and check them! This also helps to build up knowledge of the other party and yourself—important where business dealings are of a regular and continuous nature.

18

0	+10	+6	+4	0	−2	−4

Complete control is virtually impossible—even skilled negotiators are human! However, as emotion enters so reason leaves—skilled negotiators make great efforts to control and to exploit their emotions.

19

−6	−4	−2	0	+6	+8	+10

If you answer your own questions you will never know what the other party *might* have answered. It might have been different to what you assumed, and have given you some advantage in the negotiation.

20

+10	+8	+6	+2	0	−2	−4

Negotiators should be imaginative and should take calculated risks. Individual initiative is therefore important, but must be used sensibly and within limits where these are prescribed, perhaps by senior management.

21

+10	+8	+6	+2	0	−2	−4

One of the most difficult but profitable things to do. *Remember*—nature gave us *two* ears but only *one* mouth! Learn to manage silence and not be embarrassed by it.

22

+6	+8	+10	+8	0	−2	−4

One should, of course, pay attention to the *strengths* of the other party, but *do not* over-concentrate on these. Remember, you storm the castle at its weakest point! Exploiting their weaknesses can be more rewarding than 'banging your head' on the strong parts of their case.

23

+6	+8	+10	+8	0	−2	−4

Over-concentration on the weak aspects of your case can lead to under-exploitation of your strengths. Be aware of your weaknesses so that where possible you can avoid them. Concentrate on your strengths so that you make *optimum* use of them.

24

+10	+8	+6	+6	0	−2	−4

Know what you want to communicate, and consider how best to do it. The onus is on you. Deliberate misunderstanding can be a tactic, but good, clear communication minimizes the opportunity for this tactic to be used.

25

+10	+8	+6	+2	0	−2	−2

If you got this correct—well done, if it is the truth! However, if your mind does wander, you may miss something vital.

26

+10	+8	+6	+2	0	−2	−4

If you stick to your plans, and remain inflexible as a result, you may miss opportunities. Plans may need to change in the light of new circumstances or information. *Have a plan*—but be prepared to move if essential.

27

+10	+8	+6	+2	0	−2	−4

At the early stages you are likely to be fresher and under less time pressure, and therefore better able to make your points and respond to theirs. If the other party thinks price will be a problem, for example, they will try and delay discussing this until late in the negotiation. Don't let them! By all means make concessions on minor issues early on but don't let them take over the negotiation.

28

-4	-2	0	$+2$	$+6$	$+8$	$+10$

Many people feel happier at home in familiar surroundings. However, *remember*—'home' for the seller is in the buyer's office! This is where the seller is trained to operate. Also you will probably prepare better if you have to negotiate 'away'!

29

-6	-4	-2	0	$+6$	$+8$	$+10$

If you feel terrible you are concerned about what the other person will think of you—keep control of emotional factors, but if you do make a very low offer make sure it is credible! You don't want to look stupid!

30

$+10$	$+8$	$+4$	0	-2	-4	-6

Don't allow yourself to be overawed by status differences—you have your job to do and they have theirs. You can therefore proceed on a basis of equality.

31

$+10$	$+8$	$+4$	0	-2	-4	-6

Of course it may be annoying when someone chatters on, but *remember*, you must control emotional feelings. *Listen*, the talkative negotiator often gives away much of his position without meaning to.

32

-6	-4	0	$+2$	$+4$	$+8$	$+10$

Perhaps a little idealistic—after all we are human! However, it does reinforce the need for emotional control.

33

−6	−4	−2	0	+6	+8	+10

If you do get a 'No' don't be too put off. Persevere, and ask the question several times in different ways and at different times during the negotiation. If the answer is consistently 'no' with no hint of a 'maybe if' then you must probably accept it.

34

+10	+6	+4	0	−2	−4	−6

Remember, people negotiate—not companies! If you try to see how people are feeling you get a better idea of where they might move and where they will 'stick'. Feelings can often be at variance with logic but are often more powerful.

35

+10	+6	+4	0	−2	−4	−6

It may be a truism, but still valid—the man who never made a mistake never made anything! Be open and admit mistakes, and see them as opportunities to learn. If you try to hide mistakes you may land in even more trouble!

36

−6	−4	−2	0	+4	+8	+10

Imagination is vital to successful negotiation. Imagination leads to creativity—often resulting in a favourable deal that has never been considered at the outset. It also helps to avoid the trade mark of the poor negotiator—*predictability*!

37

+10	+8	+4	0	−2	−4	−6

Multiple questions can put people under pressure. However if you do use them make sure you get multiple answers! Often the other party will answer one question—the easiest—and then sit back as if all had been answered!

6

Preparation and planning

Without adequately preparing your case and planning your strategy, your chances of achieving your objectives in a negotiation are minimal. It would not be overstating the case to say that the outcome of many negotiations depends entirely on how the parties prepare themselves and plan their strategies.

If one party has given just five minutes before a meeting to planning how they will dictate the agenda, how they will open their case and how they will tackle some forseeable tricky questions, they will always out-perform someone who has given no prior consideration to the negotiation.

In Chapter 4 on the phases of negotiation we saw how preparation and planning are separate. To recap, preparation is concerned with research: it includes researching your own precise requirements and latitude for movement, researching the market and the other party's strengths and weaknesses, and making some (educated) assumptions about the other party's *ideal* and *fall-back* position.

Planning, on the other hand, is where you devise your strategy for the negotiation session(s). You imagine how you will open your case, how you will take the initiative by setting the agenda for the negotiation, how you will reduce the other party's expectations, and so on.

In this chapter we set out to improve your preparation and planning by exploring the following:

- How to set your targets
- Putting a cost on concessions
- Perceptions and assumptions about strengths and weaknesses
- Planning each stage of the negotiation
- How skilled negotiators prepare and plan
- Research: sources of market intelligence.

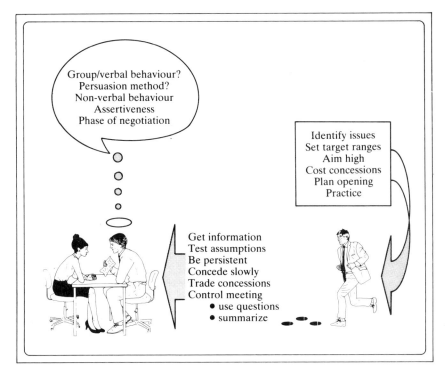

Fig. 6.1   A lot is going on both before and during a negotiation!

6.1   How to set your targets

If we don't know where we're going, how will we know when we've arrived? Wherever possible, your objectives must be quantified. Only then can you accurately measure your performance. If your stated aim is 'To reduce the price you are paying', then have you been successful if the other party makes a token movement on price? Far better surely to have an aim 'To reduce the price by 8 per cent'. While performance in negotiation should not always be measured against a predetermined target (the target could have been based on assumptions that were wrong), nevertheless in most cases targets will provide a valuable yardstick.

We know of one organization which has a highly skilled estimating department which sets targets for its buyers to achieve when negotiating with suppliers. By value engineering certain components, these estimators can accurately determine what the buyer should be paying. Interestingly, no account is taken of the conditions prevailing in the market—is it currently a buyer's or a seller's market? Yet currently most buyers are meeting the targets being set for them. Unfortunately, however, some of them stop negotiating when they reach their targets.

Being unaware of (like the buyers above who ignored the market conditions) or mistaken about some of the basic issues will affect your target setting, sometimes to your benefit. Several years ago a relative was interested in buying a bungalow which she had read was on the market for £57 950. When she had looked around it and found it was just what she wanted, she put in an offer of £55 000 to the seller, around £3 000 below what she believed was his asking price. Eventually she struck a deal at £56 000. Only later did she find out that she had misread the original selling price—it was £59 950 not £57 950—and had she known that at the time she would have felt embarrassed putting in the offer she did.

People should play a part in setting their own targets by being consulted by senior staff, otherwise targets imposed on a negotiator can act as a demotivator. If targets are wholly unrealistic they will inevitably demotivate people, but even in cases where the targets are achievable, it is important for a senior manager to 'sell' the target to the negotiator so as to gain their commitment.

When approaching target-setting, buyers or sellers use their instincts—their own feel for what is achievable based on their experience of the market and of the other party. This can be dangerous. Instinct and some knowledge of current market conditions may leave a buyer, for example, poorly prepared for a negotiation: there is too much scope for subjectivity and bias. A buyer will be better able to set targets if he researches more factual information, perhaps including cost data.

Furthermore, where sufficient information is available, objectives should be set in terms of target ranges, reflecting a negotiator's ideal, realistic and fall-back positions.

Setting a target range rather than a precise figure is good negotiating practice. As well as being easier and more realistic to prepare, target 'envelopes' give a negotiator flexibility. Golfers use target envelopes when they play their approach shot to the flag, finding it more realistic to aim at a target area than a precise point. Likewise when a negotiator tries to envisage what a good deal would be, it can be easier to imagine an envelope within which that deal may fall.

For buyers reading this book, here are some questions to ask yourself when preparing your target envelope:

- What is the supplier's pricing policy?
- Can I find out the prices of their components?
- How keen are they to secure my business?
- How large would my order be to them?

- What conditions (price etc.) have we achieved in the past?
- How strong/weak is our/their position?
- Have I conditioned their expectations, or have they conditioned mine?

To summarize, your negotiating objectives should therefore be:

- Quantifiable
- High but attainable
- Agreed by all concerned
- Supported by cost analysis data wherever possible
- Set as a target range, not necessarily a single figure, comprising ideal, realistic and fall-back positions.

6.2 Putting a cost on concessions

If you foresee that the negotiation will involve some bargaining, some give and take, you should arm yourself with a detailed breakdown of precisely

Fig. 6.2 The importance of target setting:
- Focuses on meeting our needs rather than theirs
- Provides the point of view which we have to persuade the supplier to share
- Provides datum point against which to measure outcome and success
- Retains control

how much particular concessions are going to cost you. You need to know how much it costs you to give up each inch of ground between your ideal position and your fall-back position. Doing hasty calculations during the negotiation not only appears unprofessional, it could be hazardous: you could easily make a very costly mistake. One buyer we know returned from a tough, complex negotiation with his supplier, convinced he had reached agreement for the supplier to hold their average price increase that year to 1.6 per cent. When he sat down and worked it out again he realized he had conceded to a 16 per cent increase.

Costing concessions at the preparation stage allows you to assess quickly during a bargaining session where you have, say, accepted a price rise in return for better credit terms whether you are still within your target area.

Where possible, you should also try to cost the other party's concessions. This may identify a particular issue where any concession they make would be very valuable to you, but perhaps not too costly for them. This sort of background research can be extremely helpful.

When costing concessions, remember that you need not concede ground to the other party in tidy increments or round numbers, such as 1 per cent or £100. When you move, you should move slowly and in small increments.

6.3 Perceptions and assumptions about strengths and weaknesses

Your perceptions prior to the negotiation about the relative strengths and weaknesses of your position, and the position of the other party, will be based on several factors. Hopefully, among these factors will be some factual evidence of your relative market positions, though that information (even about your own organization) is rarely as complete or as current as you would like it to be. Other influences on your perceptions will be your own past experience, what you've read in specialist magazines, what you've heard from others in the business, and so on.

So your perceptions about both parties' relative positions are based on some reliable and some less reliable sources. Equally, the other party will have formed a perception of their strengths and weaknesses as against yours, and their perception, similarly, could be at variance with reality. Whether either party has got it right or not, the chances are your perceptions will be different from theirs.

If a buyer, for example, is faced with a company showing high profitability she could naturally assume that the supplier is in a strong position; similarly, she may regard a firm achieving low profits to be in a weak position.

But profit itself is to some extent a matter of opinion. Profits can be raised or lowered according to stock valuation policy, capital and revenue expenditure policy, depreciation policy, and so on. Remember that companies achieving high profits face demands both from the tax authorities and their own shareholders, so to improve their position, companies will sometimes try to keep their declared profit down.

At the preparation stage it can be helpful to have a colleague play devil's advocate by assuming the other party's position and thinking as the other party would. They could reveal weaknesses in your position or strengths in the other party's which had not occurred to you. One American defence equipment supplier believes it has increased its fees from government contracts by 12 per cent by using the devil's advocate method during its negotiation planning.

Given below are some pointers to relative market strength. In a buyer/seller negotiation, the buyer will be in a strong position when:

- demand is not urgent and can be postponed;
- there are many potential suppliers and/or suppliers are very keen to obtain the business;
- the demand could be met by alternative or substitute materials/parts/services, etc.;
- the buyer is a monopoly buyer, or one of very few buyers;
- there are 'make or buy' options available;
- the buyer has a good reputation in the market;
- the buyer is well informed about the supply market.

The supplier will be in a strong position when:

- the demand is urgent;
- suppliers are indifferent about accepting the buyer's business;
- the supplier is in a monopoly or near-monopoly position;
- buyers want to deal with a particular supplier because of its good reputation;
- the supplier owns the necessary tools, jigs, fixtures, etc., or owns specialist machinery;
- the supplier is well briefed about the buyer's position.

We will always have to rely to a large extent on assumptions about the other party's position. When making an offer for a house advertised at £40 000, many of us would assume that the seller would be unlikely to accept anything below £36 000. We therefore wouldn't offer any less. But there may be many circumstances under which a lower offer might be accepted: the seller's employers have asked for the move and offered to settle the difference between the asking price and what has to be accepted; maybe the seller is self-employed and needs urgent cash for the business. Or perhaps the house is only worth £33 000.

One buyer fell into the trap of assuming that the future will reflect the past. After several years of accepting large increases from his transport contractor, the buyer remarked to a colleague: 'I've done my calculations, and no way am I going to accept an increase of more than £106 000 for next year's contract.' He was used to getting his own way and he assumed the contractor would ask for more.

His colleague told him his assumption was dangerous and suggested he should probe what increase the contractor was looking for. During the early stages of the negotiation, and under questioning, the contractor said: 'Unless I get an increase of at least £70 000 then the contract is not worth having.' The negotiation proceeded and they settled on a £68 000 increase.

Any perceptions based on assumptions should be marked red for danger.

6.4 Planning each phase of the negotiation

The main phases of negotiation were outlined in Chapter 4. Here we look at how to plan to ensure you get what you want out of each stage. One of the first issues to settle is the location of the negotiation. Many buyers prefer to negotiate on home ground. They expect the seller to come to them. Of course, sales staff are used to negotiating on buyers' premises and it does give them the advantage of being able to claim that certain information is not available to them: such a tactic would be denied to them if negotiating on their own premises.

Negotiating on the seller's premises has its advantages for the buyer. It provides a chance to look at stock levels, to see capacity utilization, to examine quality control procedures, etc.

The following suggestions are designed to fit each phase of the negotiation. In your mind's eye you have to envisage the whole negotiation right through to completion. What is likely to happen at each phase?   Tips on how to execute some of the tactics suggested here are given later in Chapter 9 on tactics and ploys. The issues are viewed here from a purchasing perspective.

1 *'Opening phase' issues to deal with during planning*

1 Decide type of opening and opening statements to be used.
2 Identify 'common ground' issues which can usefully be mentioned to ensure that the negotiators present at least start together (e.g. agree purpose, recap on previous discussions, common problems/opportunities).
3 Decide how to phrase the requirement for the goods or services needed . . . saying enough to start the discussion but not to reveal your total hand. Write a point-by-point summary to refer to.

4 Plan credible and realistic comments about your own needs, and credible but 'diminishing' comments about the seller's claim or position.
5 Decide tactics for obtaining and keeping control.

2 'Testing phase' issues to deal with during planning

1 Predict supplier's questions and arguments and decide how they will be answered or defused.
2 Phase 'open' questions to test own assumptions and to encourage a free flow of information from supplier.
3 Anticipate the reasoning which the supplier will use to support his position and gather facts and arguments to undermine it.
4 Plan how to find out the supplier's 'shopping list' and how to avoid revealing your own.
5 Anticipate which persuasion mechanisms will be used by supplier and prepare to match them.

3 'Moving phase' issues to deal with during planning

1 Work out the cost of concessions for each negotiation variable, and also estimate what the costs to the supplier might be.
2 Decide the 'concession increments'.
3 Decide what concession trade-offs will be cheap to you but which will be valued by the supplier.
4 Assess what personal or corporate needs the supplier has which the buyer, or the deal, may be able to satisfy.
5 Plan how the supplier can concede without losing face.
6 Make plans for overcoming deadlock. . . and adjournments.
7 Plan responses to any 'dirty tricks' which may be played.

4 'Agreeing phase' issues to deal with during planning

1 Prepare your 'closing tactics' and other actions which will help to establish common ground agreement.
2 Decide how to obtain the supplier's confirmation of the points agreed and for the buyer to retain control of the summarizing/recording process.
3 Prepare proposals for steps to 'keep talking' if agreement has not been reached.
4 Assess what information the supplier may reveal during 'post-agreement relaxation' which he is not prepared to divulge during the earlier phases.

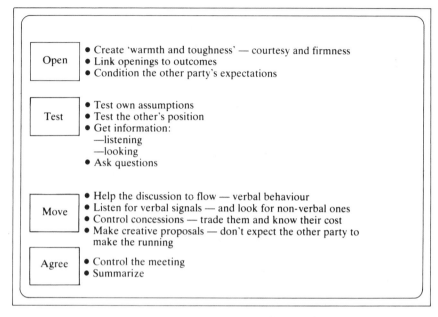

Fig. 6.3   Phases of the negotiation: what's going on?

6.5   How skilled researchers prepare and plan

Research into the ways in which negotiators prepare and plan has found that there was very little difference between 'effective' and 'average' negotiators, in terms of the amount of time they allocated to planning. But there was a significant difference in the way the two groups used their time.

For instance, we have found that effective negotiators envisage a far wider range of potential variables, openings and outcomes than the average negotiators—in fact, nearly twice as many. Effective negotiators also spend more time considering areas of common interest between themselves and the other party over which bridges could be built to reach agreement.

Another key difference that we have observed is that average negotiators anticipate discussing item A, then item B, followed by item C and item D. If the business is in any other order, they are thrown. Effective negotiators, however, are able to discuss the agenda items in any order. They do not rely on the other party following their agenda, but are flexible in their approach.

6.6   Sources of market intelligence

The necessary market information on which your negotiating targets should in part be based can be gathered from a range of sources. It should be remembered, of course, that you will continue to gather information during the early stages of the negotiation—during the 'testing' phase where you test some of your assumptions—and also at the end of the negotiation when the other party, perhaps in a more relaxed mood, may give away information which you can use in future.

Here are some sources of market intelligence:

- Internal company reports
- Published journals and business and management magazines
- Newspapers and association services
- Informal contacts with suppliers—and the supplier personally
- Visits to supplier's premises
- Published company reports and accounts
- Agencies providing specialist services and published directories
- Consultants and market-sector specialists
- Contact with other buyers
- Trade exhibitions, seminars, conferences, courses
- Industry associations and sub-committees
- Government departments and embassies
- Enquiry telexes and bids or tenders
- Information obtained during negotiations
- Other colleagues in your company who have contacts with the supplier
- Other contacts in the supplier's company (other than the salesperson)
- What you did last time!

7

Eyeball to eyeball

All your self-coaching, your careful preparation and planning, etc., will be wasted if you are unable to maintain control of and steer the course of the face-to-face negotiation. Contrary to what some believe, good negotiators are sensitive people—at all times they are acutely aware of the feel and the mood of the negotiation. They listen to what the other party is saying and isn't saying. They are continuously gauging the other party's reaction to any move they make or any refusal to move. They sense when to push and how far to push, when to concede and how much to concede. Negotiation is as much an art as a science.

In this chapter we look at several issues arising during the eyeball to eyeball sessions: first, at how you can control how the other party perceives you. Ideally you want the other party to feel warm towards you while at the same time perceiving you as 'hard to get'. In section 7.1 we suggest ways of getting and then staying in control of the personal side of the negotiation.

We then discuss questioning and listening—what questions to ask to get the information you need and how to ask them, and the crucial importance of listening to what is going on in the session, hearing and interpreting what the other party is saying, not saying and feeling.

The chapter closes with some 'danger phrases' to watch out for and tips on how to deal with the unexpected.

7.1 The personal and business dimensions
In any negotiation people act either on their own behalf or that of the organization for which they work. There is, therefore, a personal dimension which can affect the outcome, and how we manage this personal dimension can be crucial. You will generally get better results if the personal dimension can be maintained at the 'Warm' end of the scale shown in Fig. 7.1.

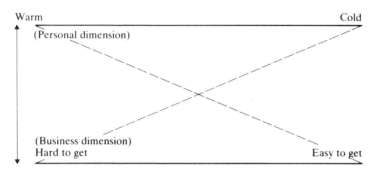

Fig. 7.1   The personal and business dimensions

Alongside the personal dimension is the business dimension—what has to be negotiated. If you are to succeed in getting the other party to make concessions and move towards your position you must try to convince them that your business is going to be hard to get, and that they will have to make some movement. If they think the business is going to be easy to get they will stick to their opening position.

We generally find that the relationships linked by the dotted lines in Fig. 7.1 are easier to manage. The Warm/Easy-to-get person is typified by the 'Morning Jim—usual order? Fine! Now let's talk about cricket' approach. Any negotiation is avoided as something which is either awkward to handle or considered unnecessary. The Cold/Hard-to-get person is characterized by formality and a distancing of one party from another—a clinical, unemotional approach.

How then do we establish and maintain a Warm/Hard-to-get relationship—the one we should aim for? To begin with the personal dimension, there are a number of factors which can have a positive influence upon achieving warmth:

1 *Interest in the* person *with whom we are going to negotiate.* Sellers generally do this much better than buyers—they appear to take a personal interest in the people they are trying to sell to. Most good salespeople keep personal dossiers on their regular contacts, recording a range of personal details such as interests, children, hobbies, marital status, holiday destinations, all designed to help them focus on the person they are dealing with. They check on these details immediately prior to calling, and look for suitable opportunities to introduce them into the conversation. They are aware that most people find two things easiest to talk about— themselves and the job they do. Buyers are flattered and 'warm' to the

person who shows interest. It is rare to find a professional buyer who keeps such details on the people who come to sell to him! Some buyers claim to carry this information in their heads. Even if they do, it is denied to anyone else if they are absent or if they leave the company.

2 *Courtesy*. This is perhaps best described as observing normal politeness—being on time for appointments, helping to put the other party at ease, a good handshake, eye contact, thanking them for coming, offering them a seat and coffee if appropriate. Keeping people waiting unnecessarily seldom puts them in a cooperative frame of mind!

3 *Being prepared to admit mistakes or gaps in knowledge*. An open admission of mistakes when these occur can be very disarming, whereas trying to cover them up is seldom successful and often results in lowering the other party's opinion of the person being dealt with. If the other party clearly has better knowledge of the subject, admit this and turn it to your advantage by asking them to explain—it is amazing what you can learn!

4 *A positive, creative and imaginative approach*. Put forward your own ideas—this can be infectious and encourage the other party to do the same. It is not uncommon, where this is done, for a creative solution to a negotiation to be arrived at which neither party envisaged at the start.

5 *Adaptable, receptive and open to new ideas*. Any new idea should be considered before it is rejected—remember the person who voices it has invested time and effort in its production and will be antagonized if it is rejected out of hand. You should try and find some positive comments to make about an idea before rejecting it.

6 *Ability to listen*. Listen particularly to the problems of the other party, and demonstrate this by asking relevant questions. Listening is dealt with in more depth later.

7 *Finding common ground*. In any negotiation there is usually some common ground. If the intention is to try to reach agreement then this becomes a firm base on which the agreement can be structured.

8 *Control of the meeting*. Control does not mean doing all the talking. Questions can direct the discussion and you should summarize each issue as it is discussed before moving onto another subject. Properly handled this conveys purpose—the intention to produce a result which is presumably what the other party also wants.

9 *Company loyalty*. If negotiating in a company context, show pride in your organization and be prepared to defend it if attacked. Moving down the 'ain't it awful' track will not impress the person you are negotiating with and can undermine commitment to any agreement reached.

10 *Respect confidences*. Where confidences are placed in you—respect them. For example, buyers who 'gossip' about other suppliers are seldom res-

pected. The person you are negotiating with will be reluctant to give you confidential information to assist progress in the negotiation if they feel this will be passed on to a competitor.

11 *Get trained!* Interpersonal skills can be learned—those aspiring to become good negotiators should be prepared to invest time in their own training and not rely solely on what they think are their own innate abilities.

The 'Hard-to-get' dimension depends primarily on one's negotiating ability and skill and knowledge of the subject. However, there are a number of other factors which can reinforce your image as a hard-to-get negotiator.

1 *Pre-organization.* If you have prepared properly for the negotiation you should be reasonably confident about *what* you want to achieve and *how* you are going to handle the situation. This should enable you to take an assertive approach and exploit the following points to the full.

2 *Tidy surroundings, free from clutter.* First impressions count! If the other party sees a tidy desk with the room set out properly, the impression given is of someone prepared. One of the most disconcerting sights is the desk with just one sheet of paper on it or even totally empty—its owner is apparently in total command of his case and needs no data or props.

3 *Know the subject.* If, during the opening phase when positions are stated, your mastery of the subject can be demonstrated, the other party will realize that you are no 'pushover'—he will have to work very hard to achieve his set targets.

4 *Clear communication.* Using clear, assertive and unambiguous language also conveys a businesslike approach.

5 *Control of/liaison with other parties.* Many negotiations involve inputs from third parties who may or may not be present. Demonstrating that they must work through you or, if present, take their lead from you will reduce the possibility of the 'divide and conquer' syndrome.

6 *Authority to close the deal.* Emphasize that *you* have authority to 'close' the deal—there need be no reference to other parties—(hopefully this *is* the case?). You then close off the opportunity to delay concluding the negotiation until the third party is present—they *must* deal with you.

7 *Use of silence.* This has been referred to elsewhere as a powerful means of exerting pressure. Talking too much can be a symptom of nervousness and insecurity—the proper use of silence indicates control of yourself and the situation.

8 *Control of the meeting.* This was referred to earlier under the *warm* dimension. Try to obtain and retain control—the other party will realize they are up against tough opposition.

9 *Reject inducements.* Avoid discussing inducements such as lunch, tickets for the next Test match, Wimbledon, etc. There is an old adage 'There is no such thing as a free lunch.' Such occasions do have their place—as appreciation for business already obtained—but references to them should be avoided *during* a negotiation.

The above list of factors which can contribute to the *warm/hard-to-get* relationship is not exhaustive—use it to develop others which may be relevant to your personality and to the types of negotiations you commonly encounter.

7.2 Questioning

It is rare that we have all the information we require prior to a negotiation. There are gaps in our knowledge that hopefully can be filled as the negotiation progresses. However, if we are to get the answers we want we need to ask the right questions and to this end we can identify *seven* different types of question. Each of them has a specific place and purpose in negotiation as outlined below.

1 *Open questions.* Information is crucial to negotiation and open questions help to extract it from the other party. They usually begin with *who, why, what, how, when,* and *where.* Such questions cannot be answered with a simple yes or no—they demand more. Of course the onus is on *you* to *listen to the answers!* Use open questions especially during the *opening phase* of a negotiation.

2 *Closed questions.* They usually demand a simple yes or no answer. They are useful for establishing *specific points of fact,* for example asking: 'Can you deliver by the 17th?' They also assist in *summarizing*—when you sum up and clarify precisely what has been agreed.

3 *Probing questions.* These are usually used to clarify points of detail and could be described as open questions directed to a specific subject, for example asking: 'What specific tests do you use to ensure consistent quality?' Use them to 'tie down' or commit the other party.

4 *Multiple questions.* A multiple question is really a string of questions asked as one. An extreme example would be 'How can you ensure fixed prices, delivery, quality and the level of after-sales service we require?' They are useful for putting the other party under pressure *but make sure you get multiple answers!* Often the other party will answer *one* part of the multiple question—usually at length—and then sit back as if they had answered them all.

5 *Leading questions.* Leading questions indicate the answer that is expected, for example: 'So there will be no problem in meeting our quality require-

ments?' Clearly the answer expected is no. 'These prices will remain fixed for a year won't they?' The answer expected is yes. Use leading questions to gain acceptance of *your* views.

6 *Reflective questions.* It is important to try and understand people's *feelings* in a negotiation. Reflective questions help us to do this, for example, 'You seem unhappy about that proposal' or 'That seems to cause you a problem.' They often appear as statements, without a question mark, but clearly demand a response from the other party about how they *feel.*

7 *Hypothetical questions.* Such questions usually begin 'What if...?' They are useful for getting the other party to think about new ideas, and are *especially helpful* in breaking deadlock situations. They enable various options to be tabled for discussion *but without any commitment*, for example: 'What if we extended the contract to two years?' or 'Suppose we made you our sole supplier?' *Creativity* characterizes the skilled negotiator and hypothetical questioning is an important part of the armoury.

It is good practice to write down the questions you intend to ask and check them off as the negotiation proceeds. How often have you come away from a negotiation and realized that you had not asked for a particular piece of information?

If you find a particular question causes the other party a problem, it can help to put the question to one side, but mark it to remind you to return to it later. The other party may think you have forgotten the issue and that they are off the hook, therefore when you do return to it they are caught off guard and may tell you more than they intended. It is much easier to do this if your questions are written down and you are not relying solely on memory.

7.3 Listening

People frequently confuse hearing with listening. Hearing can often mean little more than the fact that we are aware of noise—that someone else is talking. Listening, however, means that we not only hear but concentrate in order to understand. We have already referred to the need to create a Warm/Hard-to-get climate if we are to succeed, and listening plays a major part in this process. By not listening you may miss a vital point and thus an opportunity. In addition, not listening will naturally antagonize the other party. How do you feel if someone gives the appearance of not listening to what you are saying?

Listen also to what is *not* said. If, for example, someone says in a negotiation 'My boss would fire me if I agreed to that', or makes a similar remark, many would accept that they could not win that particular point. However, what has *not* been said is a firm 'no'—the door is still open so keep trying.

Phrases like 'very difficult' can often be used to try and deter people from pressing the point. Regarding these as positive rather than negative statements can open opportunities.

Unless listening skills are exercised and developed opportunities will be missed. What follows are three checklists designed to focus attention on this skill. Work through them with a constructive self-critical approach, marking those where you think you could improve.

Checklist 7.1 Listening—something we are generally not very good at.

Here are ten points designed to improve listening skills:

1 The essence of good listening is to have a clear mind so that you hear and appreciate the point of view of the other party. Try and put your own thoughts and ideas to the back of your mind—if you do not there is a danger that you will only hear what you want to hear.
2 If you listen carefully you will understand more quickly and avoid wasting time with unnecessary questions.
3 Other people expect you to listen when they are talking to you. Lack of listening can be seen as lack of consideration or respect, and can lead to antagonistic feelings.
4 Good listening, demonstrated by the quality of *your* subsequent contributions, can help to establish or even improve your status in the situation.
5 We need to *understand* what others really *mean* when they speak. Sometimes the actual words used are unclear, but if we *listen* we have more chance of picking up this *meaning*.
6 Listen to ideas when they are put forward, no matter how fanciful you may think they are. *Remember*, the other party has put time and effort into the idea and will be antagonized by a curt rejection. Listen for some positive element, and emphasize this before disagreeing.
7 If you *listen* to *understand* you gain a clear picture of how the other person's mind is working and can better respond to influence them to obtain the result *you* want.
8 Listening helps to identify the strong elements in the other party—their skills. Once identified, you are in a better position to plan how to tackle these.
9 Listening to, rather than just hearing what is said, leads to better recall of important information. If *you* remember and the other party has not, then the advantage lies with you.
10 Failure to listen, as well as producing antagonism as outlined in 3 above, can also demotivate. How do you feel about a superior who does not listen to you?

Checklist 7.2   Pointers to good listening

Encouraging and supporting	'I like that idea' 'I could go along with that'
Building	Adding to someone else's idea—'And we could also . . .'
Interpreting	'It seems to me that what you are proposing is . . .'
Clarifying	'How exactly would this work in practice. . . ?'
Testing	'In view of what you suggest would I be right in thinking. . . ?'
Confirming	'So what we have agreed so far is. . . ?'
Reflecting back	'It seems to me that it really all boils down to . . . ?'
Disagreeing	'Wouldn't the overall cost be more than we could stand?'
Criticizing	'If we agreed these prices for them, we would have to do the same for everybody.'
Non-verbal signals	Nodding or shaking of the head, stroking of the chin, frowning, sucking in through one's teeth.

Checklist 7.3   Effective *v.* ineffective listening

Effective	*Ineffective*
Centre of attention	
The listener keeps the centre of attention on the other person. 'What is your view of that idea?'	The listener makes him/herself the centre of attention. 'In my view that is a good idea'.
Empathy—putting yourself in the other person's shoes	
'I see why that causes you a problem.'	'I don't see why that should cause you any difficulty.'
Probing—looking for more information	
Done in a helpful, constructive way. 'You mentioned quality—what test methods do you use to ensure this?'	Follow-up or probing questions are not used at all, thus giving the impression of disinterest.
Acceptance—taking on board an idea	
The listener demonstrates a preparedness to accept that an idea or proposal is worth considering. 'That sounds interesting—could you develop it further?'	The listener fails to look for any merit in what has been suggested, and insists on his/her view. 'My view is that it wouldn't work.'
Re-stating or *paraphrasing*	
The listener re-states what has been said in his/her own words thus demonstrating that what has been said was listened to.	The listener omits to do this allowing potential misunderstanding and confusion at a later stage.

continued

Checklist 7.3, *continued*

Summarizing

The listener summarizes at appropriate stages to ensure understanding and give form and order to the discussion.	Summaries are not used and the discussion is allowed to drift aimlessly, often resulting in no clear conclusions.

Proposing

A number of alternatives are put forward and the other party asked for their views.	The listener dismisses any alternatives and proposes one 'correct' course of action.

Non-verbal behaviour

The listener maintains a good listening position—leans forward, keeps still, does not fiddle with a pencil, etc., maintains good eye contact with the speaker, smiles or nods at appropriate times.	The listener looks bored, looks away from the speaker, fiddles with pen, pencil, or anything else to hand. There is an absence of any form of acknowledgement of what is being said.

7.4 Danger phrases

There are a number of phrases or expressions which occur frequently in negotiation which can catch the unwary off guard. What follows is by no means an exhaustive list, but going through them should spark off thoughts about others which may fall into the category of 'danger phrases'.

1 *'There's just one more thing.'* This phrase is commonly used late in a negotiation just when the end seems to be in sight. The 'one more thing' is made to appear relatively inconsequential—not something which will stand in the way of an agreement—and easy to agree to. However, careful examination of exactly what is involved is necessary—an important issue may be at stake which has been left to this late stage to catch the unwary off guard, just when they think agreement is at hand! It could be the prelude to undoing the whole negotiation and starting all over again. The less experienced may concede on this late point to avoid going back to 'square one'.

2 *'We're almost there.'* Not dissimilar to the ploy above. The 'almost' is designed to make the unwary think that the deal is virtually complete, but what follows is often a vital issue. It can be used to make the other party appear unreasonable if they then refuse to concede—it will be *their* fault if agreement is held up.

3 *'Of course . . .'* There is an assumption of agreement here to what follows the 'of course'. Any disagreement can then be made to look unreasonable and many fall for this because they do not want to appear thus. Be prepared to disagree if the assumption is incorrect.

4 *'It's in your interest.'* You can be pretty sure that if someone says this to you in a negotiation, what follows is far more likely to be in *their* interest rather than yours. Look for any hidden implications in what is being suggested. Remember, in most negotiations people are busy looking after their own interests rather than those of the other party.

5 *'Fairer to both parties.'* Not as a general rule! As mentioned above, people tend to look out for their own interests and where this phrase is used it is much more likely to be fairer to *them*!

6 *'I might be able to "sell" that to my superiors.'* Where another party uses this phrase it commonly means that the deal on the table suits them; it will give them just about everything they want! The phrase is designed, however, to dissuade you from pushing further, the implication being that any alteration will mean they will *not* be able to sell another deal to their superiors. Regard this rather as an 'opening' position and carry on from there!

7 *'Very/extremely difficult . . .'* Again designed to 'condition' the other party to think that further progress is not possible. Think of such phrases in a more positive light—they usually mean 'perfectly possible but you will have to try much harder'! Remember, they have not said 'no'! Listen for what is *not* said.

This is not intended to be a definitive list of all danger phrases but should emphasize the points made earlier in the chapter about listening. Examine what is said so that you get the true rather than apparent meaning.

7.5 Dealing with the unexpected

It often happens that at some time during a negotiation we are faced with the unexpected, usually in the form of the totally unexpected question. You should be prepared to deal with the unexpected, avoiding the dropped jaw or 'goldfish' syndrome. Five suggestions are offered, but do try to develop others for yourself:

1 *Ask a question.* Avoiding answering a question by asking another is a quite legitimate way of deflecting it. It transfers the onus on to the other party and gives you time to think while they are considering what to answer.

2 *Go silent.* A very effective response, provided your face does not betray your feelings! The unexpected has probably been introduced for effect and when you refuse to be drawn its impact will be lost.

3 *Repeat the question.* This can be done in an enquiring way, designed to give the impression that you want to be sure of what was said. This at least 'buys' time to allow you to formulate a considered answer.

4 *Take up a side-issue.* This is a deflective approach and avoids dealing head-on with the unexpected. Again, you 'buy' time.

5 *'Back burner' the intervention.* Agree to come back to the point some time later, once again giving yourself time.

In summary, you must learn to deal with the unexpected and not allow its introduction to throw you off course. By mastering techniques you are comfortable with, you can deflect an attacking move and regain the initiative—and with it control.

8

Non-verbal communication

8.1 Controlling our communications

Most people would agree that the spoken word is the usual method of face-to-face communication. Certainly we assume that oral communication is the most efficient way of exchanging information ... but this depends on the sender being capable of saying precisely what is meant and the receiver listening effectively, quite apart from understanding the message.

What we say is only part of the story, and the various ways of articulating our thoughts into effective communication is covered throughout the book. It is surprising to find, however, that of all the messages we receive when being spoken to, more than 70 per cent come across visually—the overall picture which we see and, more particularly, 'body language'. Our body language includes the gestures, facial expressions, bodily postures, etc., which reveal our real feelings. The power of pictures is amply demonstrated by advertising and the use of visual aids in business presentations.

> *A picture is worth a thousand words.*

A recent experiment proved the power of the visual aspect of communication. Three groups of people were asked to watch, simultaneously, a cookery demonstration. The object was to see which group after the exercise remembered most of what had taken place. One group was charged with making copious written notes as the demonstration proceeded. The second group was asked to make only general notes under key headings. The third took no notes–they watched full-time.

After the demonstration the individuals in each group were required to 'reconstruct' the recipe based on what they remembered, referring to their notes if taken. Those with no notes produced by far the best results. They had visual images in their mind which supplemented what they had heard.

If we can look at a person's non-verbal behaviour and recognize the messages signalled in the body language then we are suddenly in touch with a significant amount of extra, and often revealing, information.

Why revealing? Researchers find that body language stems from the subconscious or natural level and therefore more accurately reflects the true nature of our feelings and thoughts. At times we find it difficult or undesirable to express verbally what we really feel. Perhaps we are embarrassed, confused or reluctant to offend or upset other people. The words we then use fall short of expressing what we really mean and so the communication is not totally valid. At other times we deliberately conceal our feelings in order not to give an advantage to the other party. Because we use rational thought to determine what we say and to whom, the spoken word is not always a true indicator of the real nature of things—in short, it can often be both inaccurate and inefficient as a form of communication. Furthermore, body language is extremely difficult to control and, if observed carefully, can be even more useful in indicating the true feelings of the other party.

Sigmund Freud wrote that 'the subconscious of one human being can react upon that of another without passing through the conscious.' The body language of one person can provoke a favourable or unfavourable reaction in another without either being consciously aware of what has happened. All of us have at some time met someone towards whom we have taken an instant dislike, or of whom we are highly suspicious. Often we can find no logical reason for our reaction and explain it as just 'a feeling' or 'a hunch'. Similarly we meet people to whom we have immediately warmed and with whom we quickly feel comfortable and at ease. Sometimes someone whom we know well does not appear to be his or her normal self and their protestations that everything is fine leave us unconvinced.

What is happening in all the above situations is that we are aware of the other person's body language. The signals are being conveyed into our subconscious and tell us that all is not as it appears on the surface. And when verbal and non-verbal behaviour are not in line with each other (i.e. are said to be 'not congruent') the result is suspicion and disbelief.

This chapter explains the significance of the many frequently used gestures or signals which are the vocabulary of body language. Fluency in body language, at least in understanding it, can only come from daily practice at observation. Opportunities abound: airports, pubs, parties, lectures, queues. . . any place where people are gathered produces a rich variety of non-verbal messages. Try turning down the sound of your television set and observe the gestures of newsreaders or interviewers. . . and imagine what they are saying from the way they are acting. Practice analysing your own body-language when you are in different moods. It is only when such gestures are brought out of the subconscious that their meaning can be recognized and the signals thus used as a valuable indicator of a person's inner self.

BODY LANGUAGE IN NEGOTIATION

Nieremberg and Calero in their excellent book *How to Read a Person Like a Book* (Thorsons, 1984) state that: 'Our own awareness of non-verbal communication was an outgrowth of our interest in developing and teaching the art of negotiating. . . We found that verbal exchange does not operate in a vacuum, rather it is a complex process involving people, words and body movements. It was only by considering these elements together that we could follow the progress of negotiation.'

The personal element can never be removed from a negotiation. If it could be then 'negotiations' could take place with a computer facing us across the table! We also need to be aware of the reaction that we are evoking from others. Fluency in interpreting body language has an advantage in the following situations:

- Salespeople are trained to conceal their feelings where necessary. A smile and reassuring words may be hiding annoyance, aggression and impatience. Analysing the signals could tell us what is genuinely felt and allow us to react accordingly.
- The success of a negotiation can be helped by the warmth of feeling between the two parties. If we perceive someone to be unfriendly or aggressive we often react accordingly and the meeting degenerates. Maybe, however, it is you who has been conveying unfortunate messages and precipitating the other's reaction.
- The aware negotiator can see if he is being received in a positive or negative manner, producing interest or boredom, etc. By reading the other person's signals and becoming aware of their true state of mind enables a change of approach to be made if necessary. For example, simultaneous use by both parties of the same method of negotiation can often produce deadlock (my logic versus your logic, call my bluff, etc.) unless one party can recognize the signs of frustration in the other and change tack accordingly.

8.2   Some initial practice in non-verbal behaviour

The dilemma is that the communication method having the biggest impact on the 'listener' is also the one where people are least proficient. . . in sending or receiving non-verbal signals. Many negotiators miss vital clues by not looking at people. Maybe this is due to nerves, disinterest or because of one's culture. Next time you are in a bus, train or lift, observe where people look. It is out of the windows, at their feet, at the floor indicator, at other people's newspapers (and don't we feel embarrassed when we are caught at it!)—in short, they look anywhere so long as it is not at fellow passengers. So, look. . . and learn.

What about sending non-verbal messages? For all but trained actors this is most difficult and will seldom appear to be credible. However, with practice, important verbal messages can be dramatically reinforced by supporting actions. The key is to *feel* what you are saying.

GESTURE CLUSTERS

Even though a non-verbal message 'speaks volumes' there is the ever-present danger of misinterpreting an isolated signal—maybe to the cost of the negotiation as a whole. Yes, observe each individual gesture but as part of a 'cluster' rather than in isolation. Considered alone, the one gesture may seem incongruous in the context of what came before or after it.

Suppose the other party laughs nervously, accompanied by a wiping of the brow, shifting in the seat and wringing of hands. Taken in isolation, the laughter implies happiness or satisfaction with what is going on. However, taken as part of the whole cluster of gestures the behaviour clearly signals anxiety, worry and concern. A gesture cluster can thus be defined as 'a set of apparently unrelated non-verbal signals which taken together convey a consistent message'.

Sometimes, gestures are incongruous with the accompanying spoken word. In this case, ask questions to obtain further information which will help you to validate your interpretation of the body language.

PRACTICAL WORK

1 Think of four different people:
   • one being warm towards you;
   • one who shows hostility;
   • one who is submissive;
   • one who attempts to dominate.
2 Write a pen picture of each of them:
   • their tone of voice;
   • set of the eyes;
   • do they listen;
   • how near to you do they come;
   • what do they do with their hands.

3 Now compare your findings with those in Table 8.1. This shows gesture clusters which go with the four forms of behaviour described.

Table 8.1   Non-verbal communication: gesture clusters

Warm Relaxed tone of voice	*Submissive* Meek/quiet tone of voice
• Sympathetic gestures • Proximity—similar body postures • Smiles • Expansive gestures	• Allowing interruptions • Head down • Downcast eyes • 'Handwashing' and face touching
Domination Controlling tone of voice/loud	*Hostile* Harsh tone of voice
• Ignoring responses • Interrupting • Close proximity • 'Stabbing' fingers and other forceful gestures	• Aggressive posture • 'Set' mouth • Staring eyes • No feedback following what the person is saying—smiling, etc. • Clenched fists

8.3   Non-verbal signals in more detail

The non-verbal picture is a big one. Perhaps the closest focus is on the eyes, then the face, head, hands, the body (be it seated or on the move) . . . even the general appearance of the individual and his or her surroundings if their influence is imprinted on them. (These 'environmental' factors are dealt with later.)

EYE CONTACT

Michael Argyle in *The Psychology of Interpersonal Behaviour* (Penguin, 1983) maintains that most of us look directly at other people between 30 per cent and 60 per cent of the time while listening. More eye contact than this indicates greater interest in the person than in what he or she is saying. Lovers and fighters often demonstrate this high percentage of eye contact. In negotiation, make your point then keep silent while maintaining direct eye contact with the other party. You will feel the tension but not nearly to the extent that the other party feels under pressure. Wait for them to 'crack' first.

Less eye contact will occur when we are feeling uncomfortable or guilty. Policemen and lawyers are working on this principle when they persistently look at the suspect or defendant. Notice too that buyers will often not look directly at a seller when asking for a concession. This usually makes it much easier for the seller to evade the issue or reply in the negative. As a tool, consciously look away from a speaker when you have lost interest in what they are saying . . . they will soon stop talking.

EYEBROWS

When lowered, one is usually frowning. This may signify worry, criticism or disagreement. But look for supporting evidence to make up the cluster. The frown may simply mean concentration or puzzlement. Raised eyebrows usually indicate surprise or disbelief. One raised eyebrow suggests an element of suspicion or challenge.

MOUTH

When the mouth drops open this can suggest either astonishment or surprise . . . or may simply be a gesture of relaxation. Tightened lips indicate a defensive mode, while a rebellious streak can be identified by a thrusting out of the chin.

HEAD

There are three main positions for the head. If held straight up this indicates a neutral attitude—listening hard and evaluating which way to go. Small nods acknowledge that the information is being received but do not necessarily signify agreement. Tilting the head to one side signals a developing interest. Tilting *and* nodding is a powerful combination which encourages the speaker to keep going . . . and maybe give the game away! Be ready, however, with the closed questions as and when you want to terminate the speech.

A downcast head could mean a problem. Basically the gesture signals evaluation but with negative overtones leading perhaps to submission. The problem is that you cannot see their eyes and are short of the information that they may send. More important is that they are not receiving your non-verbal signals, however warm they may be, so the communication may be near to breakdown. Say or do something which gets them looking at you again.

SMILE

Although we tend to associate smiling with happiness, there are many different kinds of smile. The grimace, the wry, resigned, sardonic or coy smiles—all represent very different emotions, particularly when linked with other associated gestures.

HANDS

The hands are used in many gestures, as will be seen later. One important gesture, however, which warrants individual attention is that of shaking hands.

This custom varies from country to country. In France, for example, it is usual to shake hands upon entering and leaving a room with all those present. In the UK, handshaking tends to be reserved for business acquaintances, introductions and meetings with people we have not seen for some time. Handshakes themselves vary enormously from person to person. The employer who shakes hands with palm facing downwards is demonstrating his superiority over his employee. The tight grasp of the hand and vigorous pumping of the arm suggests confidence, aggression and sometimes over-familiarity.

Perhaps the limp handshake is the one which is most disliked. Usually it is telling us to keep our distance and is advocating non-involvement.

THE BODY—SEATED

The seated body transmits perhaps the most easily read of non-verbal signals. A person reclining in a chair with feet on desk is clearly relaxed. The reasons why are almost incidental . . . it may be that they feel in total command of the situation and can ease off, or perhaps they regard your presence as being more of a social occasion rather than to do with business which needs to keep them on their toes. Whatever the reason, they show a lack of concern and do not feel threatened. They will take some moving from their position . . . almost literally!

Crossed legs and crossed arms shout 'resistance': 'Try and move me from my position if you can, my mind is closed.' Be careful, however, and look for other signals (e.g. eye contact). They may be sitting like this merely because they have been seated for a long time and are feeling uncomfortable.

Contrast this with the person leaning forward, knees and hands apart— here is openness. They are eager to reach agreement, at least to start with, but watch for the change of behaviour (e.g. to crossed legs or averted gaze which signify that they feel they have tried hard enough to persuade you but have now given up). Other gestures in the cluster are important—the other party's knees and hands may be open but he is perched on the edge of the chair. You are about to lose him so do something about it! Change the topic to re-arouse interest or terminate the discussion on your initiative.

Midway between the contrasting styles above is the 'leg-lock' position. As with fully crossed legs, one foot (e.g. the left foot) is in contact with the floor but the other leg is only part way to being fully crossed—the right ankle rests on the left knee. This usually indicates an argumentative or competitive frame of mind, but is not necessarily a negative sign. The other party is evaluating what you say (in a way, the half crossed leg is hovering between 'Shall I go or shall I stay?') so the right approach for you now is to ask for their opinion.

THE BODY—WALKING

Even from a great distance we can often recognize someone we know well from the way they walk. We all have our own individual and distinctive walk, but pace, stride, length and posture seem to change according to emotion. Dejection and misery are often illustrated by shuffling feet, bowed head and hands in pockets.

A purposeful attitude is demonstrated by the head held high and arms swinging. A slow walk with hands clasped behind back and head down suggests contemplation and thinking.

ATTITUDES AND GESTURE CLUSTERS

Observation of gesture clusters can indicate fairly accurately the current attitude or mood held by someone. Moods can change fairly rapidly and an awareness of body language can help us to identify when this change occurs, analyse the possible reasons for it and react accordingly. A buyer may appear uncooperative and defensive towards a seller at the beginning of a meeting, but when the body signals start to appear more relaxed, the seller should recognize the change in the buyer's level of interest and attempt to close the sale.

It is beyond the scope of this book to attempt to consider every mood or attitude and its related gesture clusters, but described below are some of the more common and observed body signals which indicate the inner feelings.

Positive attitudes

1   Confidence   This is most often recognized by a combination of any of the following gestures:

- An erect stance or sitting position
- Plenty of eye contact
- Leg resting over the arm of the chair
- Feet propped up on a desk
- Leaning back in a chair with hands clasped behind head
- 'Steepling' or 'pyramiding', i.e. the hands effect a praying position but with only the tips of the fingers and thumbs touching. A high steeple indicates a smug or egotistical attitude whereas a lower steeple is less blatant.

2   Cooperation/willingness/relaxation
- Head is inclined to one side
- Body leans forward in chair
- Jacket or coat is unbuttoned

- Palms of hands are opened and upturned
- Sits at right angles to or directly alongside other person. This orientation of the body can help a seller to gain a buyer's confidence *but* if the buyer is still feeling defensive, he may feel threatened by this invasion of his 'body space' and actually start to back away.

3 Readiness/expectancy
- Subject starts to move in closer to other people
- Speaks confidentially
- Hands rest on hips
- Arms are spread, gripping the table
- Sits on the edge of the chair
- Palms of hands rubbed on thighs
- Knees are placed apart
- Snaps fingers
- Strikes palm of hand with a clenched fist
- Rubs palms of hands together.

4 Open-mindedness
- Sits towards front of chair
- Head is raised
- Knees placed apart
- Legs are uncrossed.

5 Interest/evaluation/contemplation
- Head is raised
- Chin is stroked slowly
- Head is tilted
- Hand is raised to the cheek
- Pinches the bridge of the nose
- The arm of spectacles are placed in the mouth
- Spectacles are slowly removed and cleaned—this particular gesture is often used when playing for time.

6 Acceptance
- The hand placed on the chest signifies loyalty, honesty and devotion.

7 Dominance/superiority/aggression
- Hands are clasped behind the head
- The head is well back
- Legs are extended

- Ankles are crossed
- Feet resting on a table or over the arm of a chair
- Sitting with the back of the chair between the legs—straddling the chair
- Holding the lapel of a jacket
- Coat is buttoned
- Hands are placed in pockets with thumbs pointing outwards.

Negative attitudes

1 Frustration
- Rubs the back of the neck
- Fingers are run through the hair
- Breaks a pencil in two
- Breaths are short
- Hands are clenched or wrung
- One index finger is pointed.

2 Anxiety/nervousness
- The throat is cleared
- Fidgets in the chair
- Tugs at earlobe
- Hands cover the mouth whilst speaking
- Fingers tie, cuff-links, rings, etc.

3 Boredom
- Drums fingers on table
- Taps feet
- Ballpoint pen continually clicking
- Head rests in hands and eyes droop
- Doodles on a pad
- The blank stare—the subject is almost asleep with eyes open, illustrated by lack of blinking.

4 Defensiveness/non-acceptance
- Arms are tightly folded high on the chest
- Ankles are locked
- The head is down on the chest
- Twiddles with earlobe or nose—in a speaker these two gestures can signify exaggeration or even lies
- Coat is buttoned
- Fists are clenched

- Legs are crossed
- Hands grip the arm of a chair.

8.4   Objective use of non-verbal behaviour in negotiation

The previous section has concentrated on interpreting signals received from the other party. What non-verbal signals can the determined negotiator send to reinforce the spoken word? The list below provides some options depending on the desired objective.

Objective	*Body language*
1 At opening phase, to create warm atmosphere conducive to reaching agreement:	• Warm, firm handshake • Smile • Open expansive arm gestures • Gesture with the coffee pot etc. • Unbutton or take off jacket • Join them on same side of table • Sit at same level • Lean forward, open posture.
2 At testing phase, to keep them talking:	• Head tilted, chin in hand • Nod and 'grunt' occasionally • Spectacles off (providing you can still see to pick up the signals!) • Smile encouragingly • Hands held in front of you, palms towards you in a 'come on' gesture.
3 To signal disagreement:	• Shake head, purse lips • Cross arms, half turn away • Hands held in front of you, palms towards other party in a 'push away' gesture.
4 To force closure—positive:	• 'Get round something' on the table, e.g. start writing the headings for the agreement, or draft out an order.
—negative:	• Close books, collect up papers • Stand up, prepare to go.

8.5   Some cautions—the right signals but the wrong interpretation

Although every gesture conveys a message you should always try to find 'the second right reason why the signal is given' before attaching significance to it as regards the negotiation. Look for confirmation from other supporting gestures. The following also influence non-verbal behaviour.

1 *Personal idiosyncrasy.* We all have our own individual gestures which remain personal to ourselves and are often habits retained from childhood.
2 *Disability.* Physical discomfort or disability may produce a gesture which would otherwise have a totally different significance. The frown may merely be due to a headache, not signalling disagreement.

To illustrate, not so long ago a heavy industrial relations negotiation was under way between a management team and their trade union counterparts. One of the managers had only a small part to play at the outset and was now rather bored with what was going on, especially as deadlock appeared to be approaching. Without thinking, he stood up in order to stretch his legs. To his astonishment the trade union leader begged him to sit down and offered a concession. The union man has wrongly assumed that the other was about to 'get up and go' and offered the concession to break the deadlock and get things moving again!

3 *Foreign culture.* Although many gestures are international (e.g. the thumbs up) there are nevertheless different interpretations that can be placed on gestures according to local custom. Sticking out one's tongue is rude in Europe but indicates embarrassment in Southern China. It is difficult to rid ourselves of gestures acquired through our culture. Indeed, during World War II, observation of non-verbal gestures led to the recapture of many an escaped prisoner.
4 *Country or town?* City folk stand nearer to people than do those born and bred in the space of the countryside. Similarly, people from crowded countries (e.g. Japan) get closer to others than do those from sparsely populated areas (e.g. parts of the USA).

This touches on the significant subject of 'personal space', territories and zones. All that need concern us here is the so-called 'intimate zone'—people between 6 and 18 inches away from you may not be in physical contact but their presence can definitely be 'felt'. Elsewhere in this book we refer to the PDT tactic—'physically disturb them'. It works when the other party invades your personal space with the result that, at worst, you feel intimidated and, at best, your thoughts are in a whirl wondering how to cope with the situation. Either way you are no longer in control of the negotiation.

If someone comes too close, or not close enough, do not immediately conclude that they are either attempting to dominate or are afraid of you. They may simply be taking the space to which they are accustomed.

8.6 What does your office environment say about you?

So far this chapter has concentrated on individual behaviour, but your office environment and personal appearance will have as much to say about you as does your body language.

The tidy, uncluttered desk, in-tray with only a few papers in it . . . perhaps more in the out-tray, pictures, certificates, charts on the wall, absence of boxes on the floor, calendar turned to the current month: all these speak volumes about your efficiency and professionalism. Photographs of family denote an area of interest which is 'on show' and perhaps inviting comment, as would pictures or mementos about an important project or conference with which you were involved.

Talking about these artefacts may well relate to your 'satisfiers' (see Chapter 11 on negotiating overseas). Therefore, don't be surprised if they stimulate questions from the other party as part of their attempt to develop rapport, but don't forget your intended strategy and posture as a result of being put at your ease and off guard. Look out for these non-verbal signals when you are visiting the other party. They may make ideal subjects for conversation during the opening phase and provide a welcome change from talking about the weather or your journey.

Personal appearance is equally important but it's a personal matter and we will leave it to you. Recognize, however, that what is an acceptable style of dress in one country (company even) may be unsuitable elsewhere, or at least may convey the wrong impression. This is not to advocate that a Westerner should adopt flowing robes when in the Middle East, but instead to highlight the subtle differences in dress of the same type. For example, the Scandinavian man's suit will look far too casual to the London businessman and may well convey to the latter, wrongly, that his visitor is not taking the business seriously enough.

The point of this section is to emphasize that, even when your body language is silent (if that were possible), then you and your personal surroundings project an image (easy?, tough?, cold?, warm?) to the other party. The only choice open to the skilled negotiator is to manage that image so that it makes the intended impact—and not to let matters look after themselves.

8.7 When the other party has reached their limit—non-verbal clues

Perhaps the most important questions negotiators ask themselves are 'Did I get the best possible deal?' 'How do I know if the other party went as far as they could go?' There is no formula which predicts this but we believe that a large part of the answer can be found in watching the other's body language.

A colleague of ours was recently buying a house for an aged relative but, being out of town, his wife was handling the negotiations while he was away.

They were interested in two different houses and so two deals were on the table, house A being much more expensive than house B. Negotiating targets for each had been set and, armed with this knowledge, the wife was ready when she received a visit from vendor A demanding a final offer because he wanted to complete the deal. She had not met the vendor before and unknowingly confused him with vendor B. Sticking to the strategy agreed with her husband she offered a price just below the limit for house B and, after much heart searching, the vendor agreed. Husband returns home and the mistake is realized—they had bought the more expensive house far more cheaply than their wildest dreams would allow, and 'in all credibility' they would never have set their price target for house A that low.

What had happened? The wife's total behaviour signalled confidence that she was within her set limit (albeit the wrong one) whereas if she had knowingly 'tried it on' her non-verbal behaviour would have signalled that she was not sure of the outcome. Perhaps her manner would have been a shade less assertive, a 'how about if I offered . . . ?' tone of voice.

The conclusion we have derived from this and other observations is that body language changes when one person's final limit is reached and the other party is still pushing. The pressured party looks just that: they may begin to perspire, the face colours up, breathing may become faster and shallower, feet start shuffling and the hands play nervously with papers. That's the point to capture what is already on offer. To push any further is to push the other party away from the negotiating table . . . they would realize they would have to go farther than they were prepared to go, so *they* would get up and go!

8.8. Summary

- Non-verbal behaviour, or body language, communicates far more powerfully than the spoken word. The problems are that it is difficult to read and to control. Body language therefore signals our innermost feelings which we may try to mask by what we say.
- In communication, seeing is more important than hearing. What you see will corroborate the verbal message—and may also convey new information. If the verbal and non-verbal behaviour does not match, then go carefully and be prepared to disbelieve.
- Too much significance attached to an isolated gesture may lead to the wrong conclusion. Look for clusters of related gestures and believe what the cluster tells you.
- A key message can be dramatically reinforced by supporting gestures which are consistent with it.
- The chapter provides a vocabulary of body language signifying both posit-

ive and negative attitudes. Gesture clusters are also proposed to enable you to achieve certain objectives in negotiation.

- Your personal appearance, and that of your office environment, also have a lot to say about you. Manage the situation—don't trust to chance.
- Watch for the change in non-verbal behaviour, when the body language says 'I've gone as far as I can go.'

9

Tactics and ploys in negotiation

The Oxford dictionary defines tactics as:

1 A procedure calculated to gain some end
2 Skilful devices
3 The art of disposing forces.

What follows is a description of a number of tactics which can be used in negotiations, but they need to be used with discretion.

If we look more closely at the dictionary definitions a number of key words can be identified. The word 'calculated' implies care in the choice of those approaches to be used, and we also need to consider the timing of their use. The word 'skilful' emphasizes the need for expertise acquired through practice and experimentation, and the word 'art' suggests that training and experience are needed to be able to make optimum use of the tactics and ploys available to you.

No general rules can be laid down about tactics. Each negotiation must be considered separately before you decide which tactics are appropriate. It is equally essential to consider the personalities and approaches of the other party or parties to the negotiation—as has been stated earlier, *people* negotiate, not companies. A particular tactic will work better on some people than others. The same tactics will work differently on the same person in different circumstances or at different times.

The list of tactics which follows is not definitive—readers may well have others of their own. If this is the case, write them down and try to be objective about those you use successfully and those you use less well. Because these tactics and ploys are going to be used on *people*—whose personalities vary enormously—it is essential to study the *person* you are going to negotiate with. In buyer/seller situations, sellers have traditionally been better

94

equipped—they understand the need to know the *person* they are going to negotiate with. Most sellers keep detailed notes on their customers, listing likes and dislikes, interests, family details, together with a pen-picture of each customer's personality. They are then in a better position to choose the most appropriate tactic for the person and situation. It is rare to find buyers keeping any such details about the sellers that they meet.

Study the other party, list the tactics that they use and work out countermeasures.

Above all, *do not be predictable.*

1 BUILDING BLOCK TECHNIQUE

This can be used in several ways. You may request a price for only part of your actual requirements and in the face-to-face negotiation request prices for various quantities up to your actual needs. The other party will give ground more readily when you are raising their expectations.

If you are prepared to enter into a three-year contract, negotiate hard for a one-year contract and then ask what they would offer in addition if you went to two years. Having obtained further concessions, ask what they would offer for three years. You should get even more. If you go straight from one year to three years the concession you might have got for two years will be transferred to the three year contract and the concession you might have got for three years disappears!

Some people ask for prices for quantities higher than those they require and then try to get the same price for the actual lower quantity. If this approach if used, then in a buy/sell situation the seller will feel cheated and resentful. He will feel 'cold' towards the buyer. The buyer's tactic might succeed once, but he will have lost the respect of the seller and the seller will look for ways to redress the balance in future. Moving to higher quantities than originally asked for encourages the seller—who sees the prospect of *more* business than expected and can probably offer lower prices because of these higher quantities. The seller feels 'warm' towards the buyer.

2 RUSSIAN FRONT

You hint that failure to agree to a point (perhaps major but made to look minor) will necessitate reopening the whole range of aspects previously settled. The other party either agrees or faces a much worse alternative.

3 BACK BURNER

Putting off either to another meeting or to a later stage in the negotiation an item or issue that you had not planned for, giving yourself time to work out a position on the issue. This can sometimes result in the other party repeating all or part of their case and a comparison of first and second versions can prove useful.

This tactic can also be used where it appears that a particular issue is 'bogging down' the negotiation. Proposing 'let's leave that for the moment' can prevent this happening. As the negotiation proceeds, the contentious issue often resolves itself and there is no need to revisit it.

4 HEADACHE

'Oh! no! Not today, I've got a headache!' Essentially this is an emotional appeal not to press a point, and designed to make the other party feel it would be unreasonable to do so. Who likes to be thought unreasonable?

5 LINKING ISSUES

This is a very useful tactic but it needs careful planning. It is essentially a way of creating movement by establishing a link between issues which had previously been separate. To introduce a 'contingent relationship' between two issues on which each side wants a settlement is a prime means of getting movement where there is apparent deadlock.

For example, in buying a car the seller may be persuaded to make a further concession if you stress that if you do buy that particular model you would get it serviced at that garage.

6 ATOM BOMB/ARMAGEDDON

A suggestion that a failure to concede or drop a line that has been taken will lead to catastrophic consequences. This means using threats such as: 'This may only be a small order but failure to agree could affect all your business with the *group*'.

7 BROKEN RECORD

Repeating over and over again the point or demand you are making will sometimes win because the other party gets 'fed up' with its constant repetition, and feels that further progress appears unlikely until this obstacle is removed. It emphasizes the need for persistence in negotiation and a refusal to accept 'no' at its face value without testing.

8 TROJAN HORSE

Beware the Greeks bearing gifts! Be wary of the offer 'too good to refuse'— look for any hidden problems or disadvantages. For example, avoid following the buyer who gratefully accepted the offer of fixed prices for twelve months only to find the market price subsequently fell!

9 PRE-EMPTIVE STRIKE

This forestalls any prospect of negotiation, for example, 'I have an order here for twenty tons—give me a price of X and I will put your name on it!' This can sometimes panic the other party into an agreement.

10 CASINO

Suggest that the proposals made by the other party are a pure gamble and cannot be taken seriously. This can be done by using phrases such as 'You've got to be joking' or 'Pull the other one.' The implication is that if they *are* serious then there is no prospect of any deal whatsoever.

Remember—do this with a smile and you are unlikely to cause offence.

11 MESSENGER

The implication is that some absent third party is responsible for the unpleasant point you are about to deliver, for example: 'I'm only telling you what the engineers say' or 'I'm under pressure to achieve a 5 per cent reduction in current prices.' You cannot be held personally responsible for the statement. It can also help in putting down a 'Marker' without being personally responsible for it. You can then more easily retreat from this position without losing credibility. This third party must be placed at a level where it would be difficult for the person with whom you are negotiating to make contact.

12 DEFENCE IN DEPTH

Using several levels of staff/management before the issue reaches the final decision-maker. At each level it is hoped that additional information will be obtained. This must be done carefully so that you do not undermine your own authority. Statements such as 'Our normal procedure is . . . etc.', can indicate that the other party will have to conform to this.

Do not confuse this with tactic 27, Third Party.

13 PDT—PHYSICALLY DISTURB THEM

Using a variety of physical (non-violent) means to throw the other party off balance, for example:

- Lean across the table—invade their 'territory'
- Change the normal seating pattern
- Sit close to them
- Ask them not to smoke—if you know they usually do.

All of these are actions which cannot be taken as hostile but can still unsettle the other party.

14 BRINKMANSHIP

Going right to the edge requires great skill to avoid falling over! One way is to try and get the other party to see the edge as being closer than it actually is. However, beware of bluffing—if you are going to bluff *always* be aware of what you will do if your bluff is called.

15 NEGOTIATING BACKWARDS

It can be helpful to try to find out in advance where the other person would like to end up. This can avoid the resentment that could occur when you push someone beyond what they see as their limit.

16 SILENCE

At a recent meeting a manager had just made a superb presentation of his negotiating case to an opposing group. It was clear that the audience was impressed, but an uneasy silence developed as people looked at each other to see who was going to be the first to speak. Just as one was about to ask a question the manager began going over the key points again. This happened several times.

If he had stopped talking and started listening he might have learned something!

Silence is a void and people feel an overwhelming need to fill it. However, we must learn to 'manage' silence. If you ask a question and get an unsatisfactory answer, the best thing to do is nothing at all—demand more information by remaining silent!

Many sellers, faced with silence, will go on offering concessions until they get a verbal reaction, for example: 'We could do X'—silence—'And we could also do Y.'

Use silence but also plan what you will do if it is used on you!

17 RECESSING

Seek an adjournment to consolidate, review and re-calculate, or possibly re-shape a deal. New ideas often emerge if a break is taken preferably away from the stress of the actual negotiation. It often forces parties to re-consider their respective stances and question the reasonableness of the positions they have taken.

Recesses should always be taken when:

- Some complicated calculations have to be done
- The emotional temperature is rising
- You are negotiating as a member of a group and your act is 'beginning to fall apart'.

It is not unknown for a deadlock to be broken while both parties are sharing a 'natural break'.

A recess often results in a renewal of energy and concentration. However, used too often it can generate distrust, suspicion or frustration which will hinder movement.

18 DEADLINES

These can be imposed or agreed and can encourage parties to concentrate on creative solutions but at the same time realize that concessions are necessary. Beware that this does not lead to precipitate solutions.

19 THE HYPOTHETICAL QUESTION—'WHAT IF . . .' OR 'SUPPOSE . . .'

It can be particularly useful for tabling a new idea or to help break deadlock. Matters can be discussed without the fear of commitment. The hypothetical question can, however, be a two-edged sword, depending where it is used in a negotiation. If used during the exploratory/testing stage it can open up useful alternatives and help shape a deal. If used late in the process, when the basic framework of a deal has been constructed, it can cause frustration since one or other party may see it as a backward rather than a forward step, breaking the framework and implying that the process has to start again.

20 'WHY'

Never be afraid to challenge the other party, especially at the earlier stage when positions are being defined. Where you are involved in an ongoing relationship you will acquire the reputation of someone who demands a well-presented case. The more detail put forward, the greater the opportunity to find a flaw which can be exploited to your advantage.

Use the 'Why' tactic judiciously—if used too often to challenge every new idea or proposal it can cause frustration and inhibit the other party from putting forward alternatives. If you do ask 'Why' you may get some very good reasons which are difficult to refute, so you should plan for this eventuality.

21 TAKING THE TEMPERATURE

An informal meeting or contact can be used to test for views, positions, sensitivities, etc. Be careful to define the purpose of such a meeting—do not reach a formal settlement informally!

22 PERSONAL FAVOUR

Essentially this is an emotive stance. Emphasize the trouble you personally went to for the other party, e.g. 'I had to work hard to get the engineers to even look at your product' or 'I had to make special arrangements to get your invoices paid in the time you wanted.'

Some door-to-door sellers use this, e.g. 'I only need to sell one more to win our competition.' The point is made that to ask for more or to refuse to buy would be unreasonable.

23 DUMBSTRUCK

Look astonished or even horrified, but *say nothing!* This puts the onus on the other party to explain or even excuse what has been said, weakening their case and also giving you time to think. More emotion is used here than in just remaining silent.

24 GUILTY PARTY

Make the other party feel guilty by suggesting that they are breaking some code or agreement, or that they are refusing something already conceded by other, more reasonable people. They may make a concession to convince you that this is not the case.

25 SALAMI

Feed a difficulty or 'nasty' in thin slices, piece by piece. This often produces concessions because the other party wishes to get away from an increasingly uncomfortable situation.

26 DUNCE

Undermine the other party's faith in his case by claiming that he has not done his homework and has got his facts wrong—he was not well briefed. If this can be demonstrated it is possible to sow seeds of doubt about matters which have been prepared and are correct, thus sapping confidence and producing a feeling of inferiority. Be careful that you can substantiate any such challenge you make or your own credibility will suffer.

27 THIRD PARTY

State, at the end of a negotiation or at a crucial stage, that you do not have the authority to make a final decision. One can 'buy time' to consider the other party's case—this will probably have been fully argued when this tactic is used. You can then consider counter-arguments at your leisure. On the other hand you automatically undermine your own position for future negotiations, and may well be by-passed in future.

To prevent this tactic being used against you always establish the authority level of the person you are negotiating with. Ask the question 'If we reach an agreement can you commit your organization?' or some such question.

28   HARD/SOFT OR MR NICE AND MR NASTY

This is a tactic for team negotiations. One of the team makes very high demands at the start of the negotiation and indicates a firm stand. Before he loses 'face' by having to back down, another team member takes over and indicates a willingness to take a more reasonable attitude, often to the relief of the other party, though the initial high demands have reduced their expectations.

This obviously requires close cooperation and pre-planning between members. If you are on the receiving end of this tactic remember that the objective of Mr Nice and Mr Nasty is exactly the same—a good deal for *them*!

29   FULL DISCLOSURE—OPENNESS

This depends very much on the atmosphere that has been created—parties need to feel that they will not be exploited by the other and it can lead swiftly to an agreement which both consider good. This is often used when parties have been dealing with each other over a long period and trust has been established.

Remember—trust takes time to build but can be destroyed very easily. Openness is demonstrated rather than stated. *Beware* of the person who uses phrases such as 'I'm now going to be totally open with you'—they seldom are!

30   'ALL I CAN AFFORD'

This needs to be accompanied by persistence or the 'Broken Record' approach if the other party is to be convinced. If accepted, the result can be a mutual concentration on alternatives to enable the deal to be made within the limits stated. Do not over-state your case and lose 'face' by having to back down.

31   'LET'S GO FOR LUNCH'

Deals can often be concluded when the atmosphere or surroundings are changed and a more relaxed and informal setting substituted. Less formal than recessing, and can be used by either party to the negotiation.

32   SIDE-ISSUE OR RED HERRING

This tactic highlights a comparatively unimportant issue so that when finally agreed the other party feels that they have 'broken the back' of the negotiation and can relax. When the real issue comes up it gets less attention, to the benefit of the party using the tactic.

33 FOGGING

This is nothing more than pure waffle, designed to confuse the issue or 'buy' time to consider one's own position.

34 DIVIDE AND RULE

Use this tactic when in a negotiation where you are facing a team of negotiators on the other side. By listening and observing you may pick up more positive or agreeable signals from a particular member. You can then concentrate on them as being more reasonable and supportive. Sometimes the team actually begins to argue amongst themselves—listen carefully for useful signals.

If leading a team negotiation, make certain during the preparation that steps are taken to ensure you do not fall into this trap.

35 CHARITY

This is an appeal to the 'better nature' of the other party. It is essentially an emotional appeal to the other party as a *person* rather than as a representative of their organization.

36 DELIBERATE MISUNDERSTANDING

This is a particularly useful ploy to 'buy' time to think after a complicated proposal, case or explanation. 'Could you just run through that again?' either gets you time or discourages the other party from using such complication.

37 RE-ESCALATION OF DEMAND

After conceding and moving towards the other party you then find they are unwilling to move and persist in pushing for more. You therefore indicate that you have moved too far already and must return to your original position or beyond. The other party will often agree the deal at that stage, fearing that what they have so far obtained may slip away.

38 'ONE MORE THING'

This can be used at the end of the negotiation, particularly if it has taken time to get this far. A further concession may be obtained, working on the basis that the other party will not want to waste what has been agreed. Use care—the 'one more thing' must not be so crucial that it leads to a reopening of the whole negotiation. However, it can get you just that little bit more.

39 THE INCORRECT SUMMARY

Summarize in a way which tips the balance just in your favour. If the other party does not object at the time they will appear unreasonable if they raise it later in the negotiation.

40 NEW FACES

Change to another team or refer to other individuals/groups. New faces need not be tied by what has been developed in the negotiation to date. This is a tactic sometimes used in Eastern Bloc dealings.

41 ONUS TRANSFER

Put the onus on the other party to come up with ideas, e.g. 'What must we do to enable you to reduce your price?' Sellers try to get the buyer's 'shopping list'. They then negotiate each item on the list in turn, finally asking for the order because they have agreed everything on the list.

Onus transfer enables the buyer to get the seller's shopping list—what the seller needs to drop prices. The buyer can then negotiate in the same way to arrive at the price he requires.

As has been said earlier, this is not an exhaustive list of tactics and ploys but should encourage readers to evolve others. Experiment with their use, but do not fall into the trap of using just the favoured few—you will become predictable and those with whom you regularly negotiate will work out ways of minimizing their effects.

10

Telephone negotiation

The telephone has now become an all-pervasive instrument—it is difficult to get away from it. Portable phones and car phones mean that wherever we are we are never far from this means of communication. The telephone is increasingly used to canvass interest in a wide range of products and services, and many negotiation preliminaries are carried out on the telephone. This poses a range of problems in negotiation, some of which are discussed here.

It has been estimated that about 75 per cent of our information comes to us through our sense of sight. But on the phone this sense is denied to us, and this appears to lie at the bottom of most problems arising from telephone negotiation—the lack of visual contact and the conditioning of behaviour which results from this. The strong case can stand up to an exchange of words but is sometimes diluted when the parties can see each other. There is not the same pressure as that created by another's physical presence.

It has also been shown that where the two parties to a negotiation were physically present and could see each other they tended to work harder to reach an acceptable agreement, whereas on the phone the stronger case—or apparently stronger case—won the day. This is a very important phenomenon and a number of reasons can be put forward to explain it. Any reading of non-verbal behaviour is impossible on the phone and so we cannot check on the consonance between verbal and non-verbal statements. Where verbal and non-verbal behaviour are not synchronous—where tone of voice and gesture do not support the spoken word—an impression of insincerity or lack of conviction is conveyed in face-to-face negotiation. In either event the point can be challenged, and probably successfully.

Signals are often present in what is not said—the road to agreement is paved with non-verbal signals—but on the phone these are extremely difficult to pick up. It is also easier for someone to lie or to be economical with the truth when there is no one present to observe them.

104

When the other party to the negotiation is physically present you tend to give them most if not all of your attention. On the phone you can be subject to a range of distractions taking your mind off the negotiation. Furthermore, supportive data cannot be used to back your case—you may have charts, diagrams, calculations, samples to support your case but these can only be used in face-to-face situations.

Most people are concerned about what others think of them—we all like to be well-thought of. When face-to-face with people difficult or unpleasant statements can be defused by a smile while at the same time the point goes home. This is impossible on the phone and therefore people are wary about making such awkward or forceful points when the other party is not present for fear of an unintended reaction. If such points are made on the phone much of their impact can be lost—the recipient can laugh at them or ignore them, secure in the knowledge that their behaviour is unseen by the other party.

Telephone negotiations usually give the initiative to the caller, since he or she knows *why* they are calling whereas the recipient may not. Be careful that you are not caught off-guard and unprepared—offer to consider a proposal and call back with your decision. The telephone tends to force closure—there is the feeling that some definite result is demanded before the end of the call which can lead to precipitate decisions. Use this if that is what you want but avoid it if not.

Although the telephone negotiation is one of the most dangerous to enter into, in many cases it is necessary and there are one or two positive aspects. For instance, people tend to use longer sentences and will talk for longer on the phone—they can be encouraged to give more information than when in face-to-face situations—so the phone may be useful in obtaining information *prior to* a negotiation, but be careful if you are on the receiving end!

The phone can be a useful way of 'conditioning' expectations or taking the sting out of a problem. For example, phoning a customer about a price rise prior to the actual negotiation can help put them in the mood to accept, if not all, then at least part. Prior advice allows emotions to cool.

If telephone negotiation is fraught with problems and even dangers what steps can be taken to avoid or minimize them?

1 The unexpected element can be reduced by using a secretary as a buffer—someone who 'vets' calls before you receive them giving you time either to prepare or be unavailable.

2 Know who you are phoning. Where there is a likelihood of frequent telephone negotiation try to find out the best time to contact the other party, and how he can most easily be found—an extension number if possible. It

could also be useful to ascertain who 'stands in' for your normal contact when they are away—you may save a call. Remember, the telephone is expensive!

3 Know *why* you are calling. There is a tendency to pick up the phone and dial before you have clearly thought through the purpose of the call—what you want out of it. Once you have obtained this politely ring off—do not allow time to reconsider. As a general rule, matters to be negotiated on the phone should be simple and clear-cut—complicated negotiations cannot be handled satisfactorily on the phone.

4 Establish facts—use 'closed' questions which require a simple 'yes/no' answer.

5 Check assumptions. Where these are made they should be *written down* and clarified. Unless you write them down there is a good chance that something will be overlooked and ringing back later to check may well result in the whole negotiation being reopened.

6 *Listen*—to what is said and what is *not* said. It is more difficult on the phone since you cannot pick up non-verbal signals, but hesitation often indicates that the other party is wavering though you may have to do more work to win the point.

7 Listen for *moving* signals, questions such as 'What is . . . /When could. . . /If we were to . . . ?'

8 Close positively—a succinct summary of what has been decided and who will do what and by when.

9 Aim high. A high aspiration level is just as important when negotiating on the phone as it is when face to face.

10 It is good practice to confirm in writing an agreement negotiated on the phone. This should be done as soon as is practicably possible.

As has been said, telephone negotiation should be avoided if possible. Where this is not possible pay attention to the points outlined above. Many organizations who are forced by the nature of their business to use the phone actually have a prepared pro forma document to ensure that all relevant points are covered. It is possible to have space on this for answers obtained which makes summarizing quicker and simplifies any subsequent written confirmation.

11

Negotiating overseas

11.1 You are the foreigner!

One method of negotiating is bargaining—and some people are said to 'drive a hard bargain'. Although the content of a bargain may be similar the world over (e.g. price, quantity, quality, etc., the components of the deal) the manner in which it is arrived at can change markedly depending on the country in which the 'driving' is done.

Consider the analogy of driving overseas in your own car. Although you may be in the same driving seat as, for example, a buyer for your company, the view from it is different—maybe driving on the other side of the road which not only feels strange but makes overtaking more difficult. The signs and signals (even the derogatory ones!) are different, as is the behaviour. In France, *priorité à droite*, although not now so common, allows as a norm behaviour which elsewhere would cause great annoyance to the driver on the main road as he screeches to a halt to make way for the imbecile joining at speed from the side road on the right.

The point is that wherever you are in the world, whilst very similar components are used to build a car, its safe and effective use depends on the driver adapting to the local environment.

So it is with negotiation. Our observation is that the five approaches to negotiation and the four central phases apply the world over. What does change is people's natural preference for one style (e.g. logic in Germany) versus another (e.g. emotion in Italy). The untrained negotiator also usually has one fall-back style which comes into play if the preferred method is not working. An American's use of power ('everything in the US is so big . . . think of the opportunities . . . go on, reduce your price!') will typically revert to bargaining if power is not achieving progress ('OK . . . let's do a deal').

By contrast the trained negotiator has four other styles to fall back on.

Despite local preference therefore about which approaches we like to use, the components of negotiating skill are similar world-wide—the big difference is the environment in which they are used.

To summarize, for you, the foreigner, when in another country:

1 *The rules of the road will be different.* You may be dealing in a country where decisions are made by committee rather than by one individual in whom is vested total authority to negotiate and close the deal. In the former it may be that the real negotiation goes on behind the scenes within the committee during an adjournment—you are presented with a sequence of positions to which you respond.

2 *The signals will be different.* The Russian's stone-face may not signify lack of interest, but merely his personal concern not to appear too friendly or too ready to accept since he is unlikely to be permitted to do either.

3 *The behaviour will be different.* The Japanese 'yes' may mean 'no' . . . yes he understands and no he disagrees. The American's drive to win a deal as soon as possible will offend the Middle Eastern negotiator who needs time—and plenty of it—to measure you up as a worthy counterpart or otherwise.

11.2   Staking out the environment

The previous section concerns matters of social and business protocol, but much more than this makes up the environment within which you the foreigner will negotiate. Figure 11.1 illustrates the influences which will bear on you.

These are expanded more fully below, and are viewed this time from the perspective of the seller/exporter.

THE SOCIAL SYSTEM

- What is the level of formality expected in terms of dress, use of first names, use of titles, etc.?
- Is business conducted only in the office or also after hours, e.g. over a drink or dinner or on a golf course?
- Do social meetings involve wives and visits home or is all entertaining done in restaurants, clubs, etc.?
- What is expected in the way of gifts?
- Do people willingly accept criticism in front of others or only in private? How important are questions of honour or loss of face?
- Are there particular issues, e.g. matters of religion or politics or sex, which are openly discussed here?

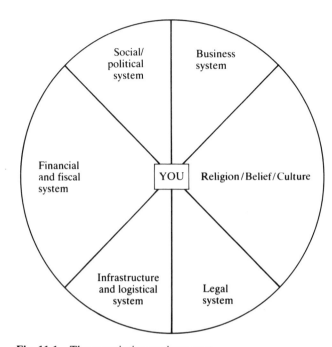

Fig. 11.1   The negotiating environment

• Do women participate in business and if so is it on terms of equality with men?

THE BUSINESS SYSTEM

• How is business conducted? Is it primarily between the principals of firms (as is largely true of the Arab world) or are all levels involved (as is the case in Japan)? Is there any real delegation of authority?
• Is everything expected to be put in writing (as in Eastern Europe) or are verbal agreements treated as binding? What significance is given to contracts?
• Do professional advisors, e.g. lawyers, play a major role in negotiations and the decision-making process as in the USA, or are they regarded as subordinates whose primary function is to 'get the words right'?
• Are formal meetings conducted only between the leaders of both teams with the other members only speaking if they are specifically asked to do so?
• Is industrial espionage practised? How careful must one be to lock papers away or even not bring them at all?

- Is inducement necessary to secure and/or carry out business? If so, how is it operated and what are the usual terms?
- Can contracts be negotiated with one firm or must they by law, or as a matter of practice, be put out to competitive bid? If the latter, what are usually the key criteria for securing the award? Is it just a matter of price?
- Do negotiations proceed in two stages, first the technical and then the commercial (as in Eastern Europe and China)? Are negotiations conducted by levels each of which will expect to obtain some concession?
- In what language is business conducted? Can documents be in two languages, one of which is English, and both be of equal validity?
- Will negotiations be with an export/import agency, as often happens in Eastern Europe, or direct with the operating company? Even if direct there may be a purchasing department involved who can be expected to have different motives to the actual users.

RELIGION

- What is the predominant religion of the country of the purchaser? (Note that religion in this context is to be interpreted as including communism.)
- Does that religion influence significantly the conduct of:
  (a) political affairs;
  (b) the legal system;
  (c) nature, or country origin of products which may be purchased;
  (d) social relations and individual behaviour;
  (e) entry of personnel having particular nationalities or other religious beliefs/political affiliations;
  (f) incidence of holidays and working hours, e.g. Ramadan.

THE POLITICAL SYSTEM

- The extent of state control of business enterprises.
- If state control exists is it organized:
  (a) centrally or regionally?
  (b) what are the limits of delegated authority from the centre?
  (c) with which state authority/enterprise must the negotiations take place, i.e. are there more than one, and if so what are their interrelationships?
- What is the extent of political interest in the particular project?
  (a) Who is interested?
  (b) What are the respective powers of those who are interested?
- What is the stability of the present regime? Is it likely to change in the lifetime of the project? When are elections scheduled to take place and is the project in question an election issue?

- What are the political relations between the governments of the seller and purchaser?
  (a) How susceptible are these to the acts of the others (e.g. the showing of the film *The Death of a Princess* or human rights activism)?
  (b) Are they likely to change if there is a change in the political persuasion of the government of either country?

LEGAL SYSTEM

- What is the legal system? Is it codified or derived from English common law?
- Is it mandatory to accept that the contract must be governed by the purchaser's legal system?
- What is the level of enforcement of laws and regulations in practice?
- To what extent are the courts and the judiciary independent of the executive?
  (a) What level of influence in practice could the purchaser or a major subcontractor exercise over the judiciary?
- What is the timescale for court proceedings?
- What means exist for the enforcement of court judgements?
- Is there any procedure, and if so what, for the enforcement of foreign judgements/arbitral awards?
- Is the purchaser's legal system such as to:
  (a) inhibit his negotiations in making agreements, granting concessions, etc.?
  (b) restrict the authority of those able to conclude, award or amend contracts to specified officers of the purchaser's corporation?
- Is there a reliable local firm of lawyers independent of the purchaser?
- Is it necessary legally to establish a local company to carry out local work? If so, what are the rules in particular on the proportions of overseas to local shareholding, fees for management services and remittance of profits?
- What are the relevant laws on employment and social security? How are those applied to foreigners? Is there a required ratio of local foreign staff? Must an engineer be employed who is a member of the local engineering institute? These may differ as you establish a locally registered company as opposed to operating, if this is permitted, as a foreign company.

THE FINANCIAL AND FISCAL SYSTEM

- What is the Export Credit Guarantee Department's (ECGD) financial rating of the territory concerned? What country limit has ECGD established?

- What is the country's debt service ratio? Has the country applied to the International Monetary Fund for assistance and if so with what result?
- How large are the country's foreign exchange reserves? On what commodities does it primarily depend for foreign earnings?
- Is the territory's currency freely exchangeable? If not what are the restrictions?
- What is the country's record on honouring payment obligations, and are delays likely?
- Can you obtain Letters of Credit confirmed in London?
- What procedures have to be gone through with the central bank or Ministry of Finance for obtaining payments in foreign currencies?
- What are the applicable tax laws, in particular on what does the liability for tax depend? Can tax be limited to work performed in the country concerned? Are there any double taxation conventions in force and if so with which countries?
- Is the remittance of the final payment subject to the issue of a tax clearance certificate? If so how is this obtained and how long does it take?
- Can profits earned by a local company be remitted overseas? If so what are the rules and procedures?
- What are the regulations on the payment of customs duties or can the contract be exempt from duty?
- Are there any other fees such as stamp duties, taxes or invoices which the contractor will have to pay?

INFRASTRUCTURE AND LOGISTICAL SYSTEM
- What is the availability in the territory concerned of:
  (a) necessary labour both skilled and unskilled
  (b) professional staff
  (c) materials for construction
  (d) constructional plant
  (e) maintenance facilities
  (f) competent and financially sound subcontractors?
- What restrictions are there on:
  (a) importation of staff labour
  (b) importation of materials which are made locally
  (c) importation of plant?
- Will the contract be negotiated and administered in the local language? If so, what is the availability of reliable and secure translators?
- What are the local logistical problems relating to:
  (a) port unloading facilities and waiting time;

(b) road and rail access to site relative to the foreseen size and weight of loads to be transported;

(c) internal air transport if this has to be by the national airline;

(d) customs clearance, particularly at peak holiday periods?

- What problems are foreseen relating to weather such as:
  (a) rainy seasons
  (b) winter, snow and frost
  (c) high summer temperature
  (d) dust
  (e) earthquakes
  (f) high humidity?

Each of these aspects outlined above may affect the programme or the design and therefore the cost of the order or contract.

11.3 Preparing for action

As shown above the total picture of overseas negotiation consists of many components; from what sources can information on each component be drawn? Chapter 6 on preparation and planning has already specified possible sources of market intelligence. The following additions will help those preparing for action overseas:

- The local branch or subsidiary established by your own company or within the group of companies to which you belong
- Your country's local embassy or high commission
- Local banks
- Your own agent
- Other businesses operating in the territory
- Your own observations and experience
- Books, journals, newspapers.

Preparation is power, and the feeling of confidence which flows from a systematic assessment beforehand, under the seven headings covered earlier in this chapter, may make the difference between a failed and successful negotiation. Why only 'may'? Because knowledge is one thing, behaviour is another.

11.4 Personal behaviour

You, the foreigner, have three roles when negotiating overseas:

1 as an observer;
2 as an individual participant in the environment;
3 as a negotiator.

1 You are the observer

Much of this chapter so far relates to observations of rituals and customs relating to the relevant country . . . seeing things through the eye of a tourist. Refer to the seven headings in section 11.2 above.

2 You as an individual . . . behave yourself!

To what influences might you be subjected in the foreign environment, to what temptation might you succumb to your personal disadvantage or even disgrace? When in Rome, to what extent do you do as the Romans do?

The advice is to fit it with the local customs to the extent that you are seen to

Table 11.1 Selecting appropriate tactics for your negotiating team

Do	*Do not*
1 Be sensitive to the local social, business and religious customs.	1 Go native.
2 Be aware of the local political scene and how it may affect both your project happening and your chances of success.	2 Involve yourself in any form of political activity or express publicly your opinion on political affairs.
3 Behave courteously and be respectful to ministers and officials.	3 Be subservient or allow yourself to be intimidated or overawed by their status or by the shock tactics they may use to impress upon you their superiority or power.
4 Prepare yourself in advance for all meetings and stay calm.	4 Be surprised at the unexpected or allow yourself to get flustered.
5 Take every opportunity to get out and about and talk to people.	5 Succumb to local temptations.
6 Have as team members those whose personality and technical abilities are likely to fit in with those with whom negotiations will be conducted.	6 Allow your expert, however brilliant, to patronize the client or try to teach him his business.
7 Be flexible and willing to adjust to their conceptions provided you can still obtain your objectives even if the means are different.	7 Be rigid and insist that yours is the only way.
8 Be careful of security of your papers and discreet in referring to people, particularly your contacts, by name.	8 Be eager to show off your limited knowledge.
9 Listen to your agent's advice with an open mind.	9 Try and teach him his business or impose your preconceived ideas.
10 Be patient.	10 Leave the territory unguarded at critical stages even if you miss a board meeting or your holiday.

be showing courtesy, respect and adaptability as a foreigner, but don't try to become one of them. They do not wish to be lectured on how much better 'our' way is, nor do they expect you to become one of them. Here indeed is your first negotiation: 'How can I persuade them to like me, to be interested in my way of doing things, and to be warmed by my interest in their approach?'

If your attitude is 'What can I learn from them?' then you won't go wrong. Some more do's and dont's for your individual behaviour are given in Table 11.1.

3 You as negotiator . . . play their tune!

You have researched and are observing the local customs. You are involved and have behaved yourself! You are about to negotiate using the principles set out in this book, but . . . one further insight into your counterpart's mind is needed. What will satisfy them? This is where we find the real differences between various countries' negotiating styles.

By and large, musical instruments the world over are designed on the same principles. The didgeridoo works because of the same physical laws that apply to the cor anglais . . . but the sound will be different and may be totally unsatisfactory to the unaccustomed ear. Our thesis is that, although based on the same principle, negotiations in different countries take a course dependent on: the preferred, and fall-back, method of negotiation, and the key satisfiers.

Feeling satisfied with a deal often depends not so much on the deal itself, but more on the manner in which it was arrived at. Time and time again on Purchasing and Materials Management Services negotiating workshops it can be demonstrated that two buyers separately 'buying' the same article with the same price label can feel differently about the deal agreed. Neither buyer likes the asking price. Buyer A has to work hard to beat down the seller from the opening position, eventually agreeing to price A. Buyer A feels reasonably happy that his efforts have been rewarded.

Buyer B, who has been out of the room whilst the first negotiation was in progress, now enters and the negotiation is re-run. Buyer B also opens with a price lower than that asked. This time the seller immediately accepts price B. It happens that price B is lower than A but buyer B feels dissatisfied: 'I started too high; the seller agreed too readily—I should have started lower and perhaps bought cheaper!'

'Satisfiers' relate to the personal needs of the other party; indeed negotiation has been defined as 'a process for satisfying the needs of different parties through mutual agreement'. Satisfiers are not territorial. The 'foreigner' visiting you brings his satisfier to the negotiating table. A trade union negotiator, being criticized as ineffective by those whom he represents, may agree to several (less visible) concessions so long as management in return agree to a key demand which he must win if credibility is to be maintained. Negotiations often reach deadlock because the 'must have' issues, or protocols, are not recognized as such by the other party.

The cost to you of agreeing to the Japanese businessman's 'must have' in order for him to save face may be more than offset by concessions he makes in return on other issues which are not so visible or important to his peers.

Being able to supply your counterpart's satisfiers means that they can 'live with themselves' as well as living with the deal agreed.

Some satisfiers are listed in Table 11.2.

Table 11.2   Satisfiers: 'What does the other person want? What will satisfy them?'

 1 Job security
 2 I have demonstrated my competence/judgement/good taste
 3 Desire to avoid risk and trouble
 4 Relief from unnecessary work
 5 Getting it all over with
 6 Looking good to others—recognition
 7 Peace of mind—'I'm in good hands; help if I get into trouble'
 8 Not to be pinned against the wall—people need alternatives
 9 Help in making a hard decision—or the decision made for them
10 To be thought of as being fair and reasonable (give them time to accept new ideas)
11 To be treated with dignity
12 No unpleasant surprises
13 Attractions you can offer on the way to signing the deal
14 Stability of relationships
15 Give me a good explanation—help me to sell this deal to others
16 Validation of self-image—some companies I like dealing with
17 Meeting a critical target

11.5   Painting a picture of the other party

A clue to knowing which satisfiers will work can be found by identifying the characteristics and behaviour which make one country's people differ from another. Overlayed on this will be the individual's personal traits and needs.

EXERCISE IN EVALUATION

1 Think of a country.
2 Write down a few adjectives which characterize that country's people. Try it as a game: suggest 'thorough, logical, efficient' and most people will say 'German'.

Table 11.3 Negotiating characteristics—the nationalities compared
These are, of course, simplified generalizations based on the authors' personal observations.

Country	Distinguishing behavioural characteristics	Method of persuasion (Natural/Fall-back)	Key needs (Satisfiers)	Key tactics
Sweden	Shy Reserved Quiet Reliable Self-critical Interested in new ideas Trustworthy Regard for quality Serious	Logic/Threat, Compromise	Reliability Evidence Trustworthy Want professional complete proposal	Logic Enthusiasm Novelty Facts and figures
UK	Formal Logical/polite Verbally indirect Appear unprepared Can seem inflexible Fair Domestic oriented	Logic/Threat (Compromise/Bargain)	Logical arguments that don't threaten Reliability Confidence Good deal for both parties Privacy not invaded Not seen to lose Non-work days private	Conservative presentations with wit Linguistics Fair offers/modest concessions Item by item
Mediterranean countries	Emotional Lively Personal Volatile 'Mañana'	Bargain Emotion	Enthusiasm Understanding	Relationships Changes/delays at last minute

continued

Table 11.3 *continued*

Country	Distinguishing behavioural characteristics	Method of persuasion (Natural/Fall-back)	Key needs (Satisfiers)	Key tactics
Germany	Logical Meticulous Efficient Formal Orderly Nationalistic Persistent	Logical Bargain Threat	Status recognition —personal —professional Save face Meet needs of the system Honour	Demand quick decisions 'Just one more thing' Analysis Mild deception
France	Intellectual Proud Cultured Love their language Class structured Nationalistic Close family ties	Emotion/Power	Personal respect Professional respect Feel that France is the centre of the cultural and intellectual world Lively, witty talk Novelty: something new or different Have style 'Over lunch'	Play hard to get Find esoteric counter arguments
Netherlands	Logical Stubborn Tidy Orderly	Logic/Threat	Personal respect Professional respect	Persistence Ponderous humour—can use lack of humour as a tactic Methodical—expect precision Push for decisions

	Characteristics	Style	Goals	Tactics
USA	Enthusiastic/open Persistent/stubborn Tough Action oriented Competitive Friendly but superficial Patriotic/tendency towards isolationism Impatient	Bargaining Power/Threat	'Win' the best deal Total cooperation Recognition Results: effect on the bottom line Business $ They want action	Time pressure Speed/action Commitment Make changes when it is put into writing Reasonable offer small concession item by item
Russia	Stalling Inflexible/unbending Poker-faced/stone-faced Tenacious Slow Quiet Always in a group Securing themselves Difficult to get decisions	Uncompromising Emotion Power–Threat/Compromise	Low total cost Exchange of goods Western presents Western currency Personal security Avoid personal responsibility Cautious about being friendly	Give as little as possible Much talk—little said No authority Time delays Change negotiation teams Obtain info/decisions without giving any themselves
Japan	Formal Yes means no Polite Thorough/efficient Lack of feeling (it seems) Competent Always in a group Hi-tech, advanced tech Commitment	Logical/Discreet use of power	Save face Entrance to market Volume Long preliminaries Long-term relationship and deal Gift acceptance	Commitment Time delays Very high offers/large concessions Linked package deal

3 Write down what you think is their preferred and fall-back methods of negotiation.

4 Next write down what you think are their satisfiers.

5 . . . also the tactics they tend to use.

6 Now think of your next negotiation with a foreigner and repeat steps 2–5. Your preparation is well under way!

Anticipating how the other party will behave is a great builder of confidence. Table 11.3 provides a reference.

Why is this important?

- Key characteristics provide clues to personal satisfiers.
- Negotiating methods will help you to anticipate the arguments they will use and also the extent to which their behaviour to you is natural (and hence unremarkable) or excited, be it interest or anger, by your own approach.
- Satisfiers are also important: you are dealing with people, not automatons, representing a company. The agreed deal may satisfy the company but the manner in which it is arrived at will or will not satisfy the person.

11.6 Summary

- Overseas you are the foreigner. Whether driving your car or a hard bargain:
  (a) the rules of the road are different
  (b) the signals are different
  (c) the behaviour is different.
- The negotiating environment is different and influenced by the social and business systems, religion, politics and law, the financial system and logistics considerations.
- You have three roles to play:
  (a) *As an observer of the above influences*: research them thoroughly beforehand.
  (b) *As an individual*: don't step out of line and become a source of embarrassment, nuisance or evoke feelings of hostility. If you respect their individuality they will respect yours. They will be offended if you suppress the differences in trying to become one of them. Don't put yourself under time pressure.
  (c) *As a negotiator*: persuasion methods and phases are universal but characteristics and satisfiers are unique. Pinpoint them.

12

Short case studies 2

This chapter comprises a further set of typical negotiating dilemmas and opportunities against which we offer you several alternative solutions. Work through these and make a note of your preferred answer. At the end of the chapter we give our view of the best solution, together with our reasons for that choice.

As with the earlier set of dilemmas, refer back when faced with similar situations in the future.

1 Filling a void

You are in a negotiation and have presented your case extremely well. The other party seem impressed but an uneasy silence has developed as they look at each other to see who is going to respond. Which of the following would you do?

(a) Go over the key points/features again.
(b) Ask them a question regarding their understanding.
(c) Turn to their lead negotiator and seek comments.
(d) Smile gently and say nothing.
(e) Fiddle with your papers to buy time.
(f) Seek an adjournment.

2 Final offers

You are selling your boat and a couple have made an offer. After the technical discussion and some exploration of price it comes to a closing phase when the husband says something like this:

(a) 'This is my final offer.'

(b) 'This is my final offer. If you don't accept it I will buy another in a couple of days.'
(c) 'This is my final offer for the boat and I will discuss the contents separately.'
(d) 'This is my final offer—here is my cheque now. It is only valid for three days.'
(e) 'This is my final offer. I can give you a cheque now.'
(f) 'This is all I can offer—take it or leave it' (in a very hard tone).

Which of these is most final and promises least hope of further negotiation?

3 Make me an offer

You are negotiating to sell two earth-moving machines. The buyer indicates that she is ready to buy but that the deal must include you taking her old machines in part exchange. The buyer asks you what your offer for them will be. As a seller what do you do?

(a) Make her a higher offer.
(b) Ask her what she wants.
(c) Make her a low offer.
(d) Inform her that the company policy precludes it.

4 When is a deal fair and reasonable?

You are buying a new motor car for cash. You have set your mind on one particular model and have obtained prices from three garages.

Garage:	A	B	C
Price:	£7100	£7300	£7295

The deal on offer from each supplier is identical in terms of added extras, delivery, colour of the car, etc. The only difference is the price. Write down what you feel would be your negotiation objective for each of the three garages. Give a separate price target for your negotiation with each garage.

5 Still apart

You are in a negotiation in which you and the other party are unable to reach agreement. Both sides believe firmly in their respective positions, and in many hours each has made only token movement. What would be the order of your preference of these six possible courses of action?

(a) Change negotiators.
(b) Offer a large concession.
(c) Offer a further small concession.
(d) Change the package and scope of the negotiation.

(e) Let it go to deadlock.
(f) Be open about your feelings at the lack of movement.

6 *Reducing the seller's demands*

You are a buyer for a retailer, about to enter negotiation with a manufacturer of electrical appliances. You want to reduce the seller's demands and final price as much as possible. Which option below would you choose if you planned to (1) reduce the seller's opening demand, or (2) reduce the final price?

(a) Make sure that specification(s) for the item(s) is (are) such that other manufacturers can meet it/them easily.
(b) Ask for a quotation before the meeting: 'Please quote your lowest price.'
(c) 'Drop a few names'—indicate that you are seeking/or have quotes from other suppliers.
(d) Indicate that you are seeking a long-term business relationship.
(e) Ask for a quotation for more than you will require.
(f) Place emphasis on the size of your order and the importance of supplying you.
(g) Ask for a quotation for less than you will require.

7 *What's in it for me?*

You have been working a long time on a major sale which, if it comes off, will considerably enhance your promotion prospects. You are very close to agreement with the buyer. He now hints that he wants a personal reward for completion.

Do you:

(a) Find out what he wants?
(b) Offer him the chance to visit your factory in Nice?
(c) Ignore it?
(d) Threaten to report him to his management?
(e) Hint at a sum of money and subsequently renege?
(f) Say you would like to help but that it is not company policy?

8 *Opening offers*

You wish to sell your boat which cost £48 000 two years ago. Based on professional advice you would be delighted to get £39 000 although you have set a fall-back minimum £37 500. Before you get around to putting it on the market a nodding acquaintance offers you £40 000. In response do you:

(a) Accept with alacrity?

(b) Accept?
(c) Ask for £42 000?
(d) Say you only want £39 500?
(e) Ask what he will pay for the extras?
(f) Stay silent?
(g) Say you've been taken aback by his offer?

9 *Enough is enough*

You are in a negotiation with a very tough negotiator who has pushed you to concede a great deal more than you should have done. Although you know the contract will still be profitable to you at the price currently on the table, you are 2 per cent beyond your brief. You think you can sell the deal to your MD at this level but the other party wants a further concession.

Do you:

(a) Concede on a variable such as packing, delivery, payment, etc.?
(b) Ask him how much more he wants and give it to him—provided you are still convinced that your MD will agree?
(c) Ask him how much more he wants and offer to 'split the difference'?
(d) Ask for a recess?
(e) Explain that you have already exceeded your brief and have 'put your head on the block'. You must therefore return to your original opening position?
(f) Call your boss?

10 *Taken for a ride*

You are staying in a hotel for three nights whilst visiting an important customer whose offices are located about three miles away. The first morning you take a taxi which costs £3.80 for the journey. You do the same on the second morning and it costs the same. On the third morning you again take a taxi, but as the driver leaves the hotel he turns left towards the town instead of going straight on as had happened on the previous two mornings.

The journey has taken under ten minutes on previous occasions so you wait a while to see if he is taking you a better way, or one that is equally quick. After five minutes or so it becomes obvious that he is taking you out of your way. You mention your destination and ask which way he is going. He quickly apologizes and says he was dreaming, but that it will now be quicker to carry on rather than go back.

When you finally arrive at your destination do you:

(a) Ask how much the fare is?
(b) Tell him you are only paying the same as on the other two days?

(c) Say nothing, but look at him?
(d) Pay what is on the meter because he made a genuine mistake?

Answers

Case 1 answer: option (d) You have done all that could be expected of you—it is now up to them. Any other alternative relieves pressure. The ball is in their court—let them play it! It also emphasizes the importance of managing silence, something we are not generally good at. But this option should only be used when you know you have made an excellent job of presenting your case, so good that there is a natural pressure on the other party to respond. If your presentation had merely been good, options (a), (b) or even (c) could then be appropriate.

Case 2 answer: option (a) Any other involves a qualification of the statement which he may not necessarily mean, and could give rise to an emotional reaction. The skilled negotiator must learn to say 'no' in a clear, unequivocal but unemotional way with no ambiguity as to the meaning.

Case 3 answer: option (b) It appears that you are virtually faced with another negotiation—the part-exchange value of the old machines. Remember the rules for bargaining: do not put a marker down too early but try to get the other party to do this. Option (b) puts the ball in her court—if she gives a figure, you can then reduce it, since it is unlikely to be her absolute sticking point. Or you could reject the part-exchange option and look for another approach. A creative approach could bring you a better deal.

Case 4 answer The figure you give is less important than the fact that it should be the *same* for each garage. The deal is exactly the same—why pay more at one than another? We must guard against being 'conditioned' to pay a higher price merely because the opening point was higher.

Case 5 answers: options (f), (d), (a) Openness can be very powerful, and can put the other party under pressure to do something to relieve the situation. They are made to feel responsible for the lack of movement, hence option (f) is the first choice. Option (d) is second: the existing package will apparently produce no result and it may be worth seeing if a change will break the impasse. However, be careful that in making a change this does not appear as a concession to the other party.

Option (a) may be worth trying since the 'chemistry' may not be right between those currently involved in the negotiation. Changing the people may produce a result.

Case 6 answer: (1) option (a), (2) option (g) If the specification is such that many suppliers could meet it, a highly competitive situation exists—if they want the business they will have to put in a competitive bid. Hence option (a).

Some buyers ask for a quotation for more than they require and then try and get the same price for a *lower* quantity. This antagonizes sellers and produces negative feelings—it moves them away from the 'warm' position and towards the 'cold'. If you ask for less than you actually require and you negotiate hard at that figure and then state that you actually could place an order for more, the seller clearly realizes that some price adjustment will be necessary. But at the same time he is getting more business than he thought. He now has more positive feelings and is at the 'warm' end of the scale. The move must be credible, however, from what you ask for and what you finally order. See tactic 1 in Chapter 9.

Case 7 answer: option (c) Remember, this is totally unethical in Western culture, and could be just as much a threat to you as it might be to him. It may be just a 'try on' and by ignoring it you demonstrate that you are not prepared to go down that track.

Case 8 answer: option (g) This is an opening offer. Silence would probably be an unnatural or unfriendly response. A better way is to say something very neutral—perhaps say you didn't know he was looking to buy a boat. There is then a good chance if he's serious that he will come back with an improved offer.

Case 9 answer: option (e) This is known as re-escalation of demand. Options (a), (b) and (c) offer hope of even more concessions—the last thing you want. By stating that you have gone further than you should and must now retreat you demonstrate to the other party that the end has been reached: they run the risk of losing much of what they have so far achieved if they go any further and perhaps should settle before you implement your intention. Second best would have been (d). Don't use (f) as it will undermine your credibility.

Case 10 answer: option (c) Again, silence will put the onus on him to make an offer. He is at fault in going the wrong way and should offer something for the inconvenience caused. This actually happened to one of us. When we eventually arrived at the customer's premises, the driver apologized and said 'How much did you pay yesterday?' I remained silent. He then said 'Was it £2 or £2.50?' The pressure was on him to make a very reasonable offer, having wasted my time. Of course the amounts were small but the principle is important—silence can be a potent weapon in negotiation.

13

Checklists for success

The purpose of this chapter is to act as a ready reference for the negotiator in a hurry. It serves as a reminder of some key do's and don'ts which may make the difference between success or failure in your next negotiation. At the end of the chapter in section 13.3 we present a contingency plan for someone who's *really* in a hurry and has only, say, five minutes in which to prepare. If the negotiation is important and you don't even have this much time then it would be unwise to proceed. Negotiate instead for a postponement, and recognize that if the other party resists then this may only be their tactic for applying pressure.

13.1 Negotiation—some do's

- *Be clear about your point of view.* Negotiation is about moving the other party to come round to your way of thinking, to win them over to your point of view. You cannot be effective if you don't have a clear picture of your own position. It often helps to say out loud to yourself what you believe to be your 'rights' in the situation ... but remember that the world does not owe you a living so you must persuade it to see things your way.
- *Dig in, early on, on a big issue and stick close to your position.* The effort of doing so begins to alter the other party's expectation of the final deal which is to be struck.
- *Work out the relative bargaining power of yourself and of the other party.* If you have power, use it carefully and gently at first. Take care that if you use power to get your own way, then sooner or later they will do the same with you—perhaps on the next deal. You will have taught them how to deal with you.
- *Try to get into a position where you don't have to use the bargaining mode of negotiation.* Never betray by the merest gesture that you are willing to

trade. Take a posture and stick to it as long as possible. Remember that only two of the approaches we've outlined involve you giving up part of your position: bargaining and compromise. The other methods—logic, coercion, emotion—all have the potential to win the other party completely over to your position without you moving.

- *Trade or bargain on the 'straw' issues.* If you have to trade do so only on the minor issues. Make these issues appear important: for example, by only trading them and never giving them away. Go through the motions of bargaining and allow the other party to 'win' concessions.

- *The scout's motto: 'Be prepared'.* Preparation and planning are important. We never have enough time. However, there is generally no difference in the time allocated to this phase of negotiation by average and successful negotiators. The difference is in the type of planning. Successful negotiators balance their time between process (how) and task (what) issues rather than concentrating on task issues only.

- *Manage your team.* If you are not alone then allocate tasks:
  (a) Calculations
  (b) Tracking concessions
  (c) Opportunities.
  Avoid at all costs the person who hasn't been *listening* and jumps in with both feet to undermine your case.

- *Make the other party compete.* Try to avoid premature commitment to their product or service. Keep them selling because their propensity to make concessions will be greater. Hiding the true quantity you want to buy is another way of making them compete. Selectivity and variation in timing of purchase will also help.

- *Recess.* Use this tactic to avoid the early close or premature pressure to commit, to consider/review difficult issues and to make even the shortest of calculations—especially when a calculator is involved. Never feel bad about it. Time the recess to maximum effect.

- *Integrity rather than complete openness.* A good negotiator does not reveal his total hand, nor does he tell the complete story of what he wants or why he wants it. A good negotiator reveals information in small pieces, as and when it is necessary. He hides from his opponents feelings about the objectives he has been set to achieve. Having said that, he must provide an anchor for the other party. If he makes a commitment it has to hold. If the other party distrusts the negotiator he will be nervous/anxious and may withdraw. He will almost certainly become more difficult to deal with. A good negotiator must be *trustworthy.*

- *Listen, rather than talk.* We are all inclined to waffle and wave the flag; we keep talking to show what good negotiators we are and to display our knowledge. If we lack confidence it helps to keep up our spirits. How wrong we are—it pays much more to listen. Listening and responding to the other party helps create empathy. The listener will be able to spot opportunities, detect problems, judge the limits of the other party's position and, when he does talk, he will do so with more knowledge, hence increasing his confidence and ability to ask good questions.

- *Summarize.* Do so regularly and not just at the end. Sum up the points you like and weaken the other party's position by ignoring or playing down those you don't like. Use it to illustrate the concessions you need—'If you can do this and this, then we . . .'

- *Lend a helping hand.* If the other party gets himself into a deep hole it can pay well, on occasions, to give him a ladder. A small investment for a larger return.

- *Aim high.* The more you ask for the more you get. It pays to make high demands. However, a posture must be credible. Too high, and you will achieve deadlock or the other party may withdraw. Very high demands need to be tentatively signalled to the other party in order to test reaction and set up expectations. The higher you aim the more likely the other party is to ask you 'why'. So have a response prepared, but it does not necessarily have to be a case based on logic. Emotions and feelings can just as effectively support an ambitious target. 'I feel your prices are far too high', or 'When you stopped deliveries in order to force us to pay your price increase you badly damaged the relationship between our companies' are powerful expressions of feeling if stated assertively. What price confidence? What price hurt pride?

- *Use the building block technique.* Each negotiable issue is a card in your hand—do not play them all at once. Play the cards singly and get a concession from the other party each time, e.g. get the best price for a smaller volume, then a reduction for larger volume over the year, then two years, and so on. Too many buyers offer 'good news' to the supplier even before the negotiation has begun: 'Before we start let me say that we are now looking for twice the volume and a three year contract!'

- *Elicit offers . . . don't make them.* Get the other party to reveal their targets, or what 'they think is reasonable'. Use the 'what if' or 'just supposing' questions if they do not respond to a direct approach. Reveal your expectations too soon and you'll never know what they *might* have offered which was better.

- *Say thank you!* Always thank the other party for any concessions they offer. This is part of being 'warm' and courteous but, more important, establishes that you have received and taken ownership of what was offered. If this is not done there is the real danger that the concession will be taken back. Saying thank you does not stop you from asking for more, but it means that you can place your foot firmly on the next stepping stone towards your goal.

- *Authority*. Ensure you understand the levels and extent of your authority in the areas in which you are to negotiate. The tactics of 'removed authority' or 'defence in depth', that is removing or strictly limiting authority, can be beneficial if not declared to the other party.

13.2 Negotiation—some don'ts

- *Don't make things easy for the other party*. People derive more satisfaction from things they have worked hard to get. Give the other party this satisfaction. On the other hand, at the end make it a little better than they thought it was going to be.
- *Don't compromise early in the meeting*. Compromise will favour the party who postures more extremely. Use it to break an impasse or bridge a 'last gap'.
- *Don't always leave the important issues to the middle/end of the agenda*. To do so is the predictable behaviour of the average negotiator, often resulting in lack of time on the important issues.
- *Never, ever show triumph*. The sting in the tail. We have all seen the negotiator who lost and said little, but seethed with anger and determined to beat the other party, if not destroy him, the next time.
- *Don't feel too successful*. Bernard Shaw once said 'Success is the brand on the brow of the person who aimed too low.' Are we successful? Was our need to feel successful strong? Was our perception of what was possible lowered?
- *Don't 'paint' yourself or the other party into a corner*. Leave yourself room. Good negotiators don't use 'either or', they use 'if and then'. A cornered animal can be dangerous. Never ask 'What is your lowest price?' 'Is that the best you can do?'
- *Don't go it alone on protracted or complex negotiations*. To negotiate and remain objective is very difficult. To have a partner who remains objective can be beneficial. Besides the obvious advantage of increased security, another person can, for example:
  (a) decide when a recess is relevant;
  (b) plot concessions made by the parties;
  (c) listen for signals—sometimes what is not said rather than what is said.
- *Don't lack confidence*. Those who have confidence will ask questions/get information and challenge positions and ideas. Why does one lack confidence? This arises from two related yet somewhat different sources:
  (a) the fear of losing;

(b) the fear of facing an experienced opponent.

Both can be avoided by knowledge: preparing your groundwork thoroughly and the knowledge that you are a trained, skilled negotiator. Lack of confidence often results from fear that a mistake might be made. It is a pity because we learn more from our mistakes. Remember that the making of a mistake is not a final defeat—it can be rectified without damage to one's negotiating position.

- *Don't get sidetracked.* The use of side-issues is a classical tactical ploy. Don't wander, unless you intend to do so. Your opponent will try to side-track you if he considers he is losing a particular point under discussion or that a telling point is about to be made against him. Be on your guard! The 'back burner' is a useful counter tactic.
- *Don't 'bridge'.* Saying phrases like '3 or 4 per cent' or '4 or 5 years' not only signals uncertainty on your part but also allows the other party to choose the number that suits them best and then concentrate on it.
- *Don't be greedy.* A negotiator needs to push hard then grab that result/ opportunity and not try for something his opponent will never give. Being greedy you risk losing all. Don't take that risk.
- *Don't move quickly.* A slow concession pattern is a trait of a good negotia-tor. Go for the most you can get and don't come off this top limit of your aspirations too easily. To do anything else signals an initial demand that was too strong and motivates your opponent to push you down.

13.3   An emergency plan for those preparing in a rush

1 Remember that *everything* is negotiable—even time. Postpone the negotia-tion if you need more time.
2 Your job is to get the other party to see things *your* way.
3 Be clear in your own mind about what *is* your point of view. If necessary say it out loud to yourself.
4 Think of a case which fits each of the five methods of negotiation.
5 Be warm and tough: be friendly and courteous, and remember there is a place for humour and for thanks.
6 Set high but defensible targets and communicate them in personal terms.

Index